PERPETUALLY BROKE: LIVING BEYOND YOUR INCOME?

What They Didn't Teach You In School, How To Manage Your Money, Pay Off Debts, Get A Money Makeover And Achieve Prosperity By 40

TOM CROMWELL

CONTENTS

The Personal Financial Calculator - Budgeting Tool	v
The Secret of Using this Book to Change Your Life	1
How to Use This Book	5
Chapter One: Take Ownership of Your Problems	7
Chapter Two: Understand your behavior and how it is Manipulated	22
Chapter Three: What You Need to Change to Achieve Your Financial and Life Goals	43
Chapter Four: Making Choices and Creating Positive Changes	64
Chapter Five: The Outcome You Need to Achieve Now, Which will Lead to Financial Prosperity	83
Chapter Six: How to Create a Financial Plan in Just a Few Hours	97
Chapter Seven: Your Financial Makeover Plan	111
Chapter Eight: How to Cut Your Spending and Prioritize other goals	129
Chapter Nine: Plan for Life	141
Chapter Ten: Achieve Financial Prosperity	150
Afterword	161
Author's Note	165
The Personal Financial Calculator - Budgeting Tool	167
References	169

© Copyright 2020 - All rights reserved worldwide.

It is not legal to reproduce, duplicate, or transmit any part of this document in either electronic means or in printed format. Recording of this publication is strictly prohibited and any storage of this document is not allowed unless with written permission from the publisher, Platinum Edge Media Ltd, except for the use of brief quotations in a book review.

DISCLAIMER

This book is produced as is. I make no representations as to the accuracy, completeness, suitability, or validity of anything contained therein. The information in this book represents the opinion of the author, based on experience, and must **not** be construed as specific legal or financial advice. You are solely responsible for your legal and financial decisions - please engage your own advisor. Neither the author nor publisher accepts any liability for direct, indirect, or consequential loss or damages howsoever arising from the information provided in this book.

THE PERSONAL FINANCIAL CALCULATOR - BUDGETING TOOL

(Never budget without this)

Save massive time and effort:

- Track your income and spending.
- Pre-configured with **21** critical budget categories.
- Calculate whether you have surplus or deficit, and track your savings.

The last thing you want is to miss critical items of expenditure that will ruin your budget because you forgot about them. I will also give you an additional 7 monster money tips.

To receive your **FREE** personal financial calculator & 7 monster money-saving tips, visit the link:

<u>www.personalfinancewizard.com</u>

THE SECRET OF USING THIS BOOK TO CHANGE YOUR LIFE

ARE YOU LIVING BEYOND YOUR MEANS AND BORROWING money to pay for it?

Do you feel you have a poor grasp of your financial situation?

Do you make impulsive decisions to spend money, which you regret later?

Does money control you rather than the other way around?

Are you living paycheck to paycheck with no financial plan for the future?

This book has been created so you can solve all these problems. To be clear, if you suffer from these issues, then you fall into the majority of American, Canadian and British people, especially millennials and now Gen-Z.

In this book, you will learn:

- About the root causes of these issues in your life and the levers of control
- How your behavior is being manipulated and how to resist it

- Why you need to recognize and change specific behavior and how to achieve it
- How to set financial goals and plan for the future
- How to make sound financial choices and drive positive changes in your life
- Specific and highly targeted actions that will make change happen fast
- How to create a financial plan and use it to meet your goals
- How to stay on the road of financial prosperity
- Makeover techniques for slashing spending and cutting debt
- How to create a plan for life and achieve financial prosperity

This book is not another quick fix 'how to budget' guide - it will help you look inside yourself and your problems. Using a melding of modern psychology with some ancient philosophy, I will arm you with the weapons you will need to seize control of your financial future and hold it against all counter-attacks. You will learn the necessary techniques and underpin these with a changed belief system to create guiding principles to better manage your life and finances.

You may have found yourself in a dire financial situation, or something may have triggered you into acting. This is again, a common scenario. Possibly you have been refused further credit due to your debt, prompting a personal credit crunch. Perhaps you have a new goal, such as buying a house or apartment, but your finances are too disorganized. Maybe you had an epiphany and realized you would never achieve your financial expectations and dreams.

Jeff had such an epiphany when he met a couple in their

60s who were nearing retirement, had only $30,000 in savings, no pension, and small social security checks. Seeing the dismal state of their finances lit a fire under Jeff. He immediately went from putting just 3% into his 401k to making the maximum contribution, starting a Roth IRA, while limiting what he spent.

Personally, I have used these lessons and principles throughout my life, and they have delivered handsomely. They worked as well when I was earning very little as they work now that I am more secure. They enabled me to climb up the wealth ladder from the lowest rung to a position of financial freedom and prosperity. However, I have not forgotten the pain, nor the lessons of watching other people's lives implode all around me due to debt and financial mismanagement. I will share some of these stories through this book. I have built up a wealth of practical and corporate financial experience, and I am passionate about wanting to use it to help other people achieve the financial freedom that I enjoy.

By reading this book and taking the time to evaluate your income, expenditure, and factors that are driving your spending, you will be able to implement the right changes to your financial habits and behaviors. As a result, you will reap the rewards of prosperity and eventually, financial freedom. This means you will be able to generate sufficient income outside of a 9-5 salary and live your life in the way you choose.

This is not the promise of a quick fix for any problem. You will need to apply focus, perseverance, and a little discipline. However, as you will see, we will not be talking about the constant need to exercise your willpower and self-control. The methods proposed in the book, if applied consistently, will generate deep and lasting changes to your behavior that will change your life.

I promise you that if you absorb the contents of this

book and follow the straightforward guidance, then you will immediately begin to feel in control and more secure of your personal finances.

"It doesn't take a lot to feel positive about money. Just sitting up and paying attention made me feel more in control. Of course, you should always cherish your friends and family first, but taking control of your finances can be the key to happiness, and isn't that what's really everything?" - Lauren Bowling, Magic Money Tree.

If you remain on this path, you will reach a position of financial comfort and even prosperity faster than you ever imagined. A year from now, you will wish you'd started today, the time to act is now. The longer you delay getting onto the right track, the harder it will become, since you will end up accumulating more debt and have less time to get returns on your investment. This will severely impede your goal for financial freedom - *having a reliable stream of income, which allows you to afford the lifestyle that you want.* Furthermore, failure to act now will entrench any bad habits that you may have developed, thus making the process of changing them an uphill task.

Read on now, and join me to begin your journey to financial prosperity.

HOW TO USE THIS BOOK

This book has been structured and written to guide you through a process of personal change. Therefore you must read each chapter in turn rather than dive around. The information in subsequent chapters may depend on the understanding you have gained from an earlier chapter in the book.

Each chapter will conclude with some takeaways and actions to be performed. To be successful, it is critical that you follow up on these actions. Once again, they build upon one another and help to take you through the process to the final steps.

You will be surprised how little time this will actually take. Most of the time that you will need will be used to gather your financial information together. To decide *(with your partner, if you have one)* on your aspirations, goals, and motivations. You should also find the process emotionally energizing and insightful.

Lastly, I would like to emphasize that this is a process, it is a journey that will change and evolve according to your circumstances. However there are more resources and support available to you if you need them, please click on the link.

<u>www.personalfinancewizard.com</u>

CHAPTER ONE: TAKE OWNERSHIP OF YOUR PROBLEMS

IN THE HIGH CONSUMPTION AND DEBT-RIDDEN SOCIETY that we live in today, living beyond one's means is a familiar phenomenon. The YOLO *(you only live once)* philosophy that pervades modern society has normalized excessive spending, usually on things we don't need and can do without. The pressure to acquire the latest gadgets, fit in with popular trends and 'keep up with the Joneses' has turned many of us into extravagant spenders who hardly ever step back to think about how we are spending our money. Due to the easy credit that is advanced by most financial institutions and other lenders, many people are quick to take on debts in pursuit of instant gratification. These debts are often taken to acquire liability goods and assets that depreciate as soon as they are purchased, leading to an unsustainable cycle of debt. Meanwhile, we aspire to achieve prosperity and retire early on a comfortable income.

When we moved to a small village, we had some neighbors who bought a run-down cottage at the same time. They proceeded to knock it down and build a large house with outbuildings; it was fantastic. I confess I was envious. They had cars, she went riding, and they had a son the same age as our daughter. So we mixed, as it was a small village. He wasn't working, but they had investments. Their life appeared idyllic from the outside, but then one day someone turned up to repossess the BMW. The whole house of cards came crashing down. It transpired they were massively in debt, and everything was mortgaged to the hilt, their lifestyle was completely unaffordable. Apparently, she had no notion until the repo men turned up, of course, it didn't turn out well for their marriage.

This spendthrift attitude has become so common that many people are never aware of it when they engage in unfettered spending. It is not unusual for even the most financially prudent individuals to be mocked and chided as being miserly. However, despite how normalized it has become, living beyond one's income can have dire effects, not just on individuals but on organizations and even economies as well. At a macro level, we have all seen the impact of runaway debt on the economies of many countries. Perhaps, the best example of the dangers of living beyond one's means on the scale of countries can be seen in Greece, whose economy nearly collapsed in the late 2000s due to poor fiscal policies that led to the ballooning of public debt. The country had to embark on various emergency measures, including debt restructuring and austerity to survive the economic apocalypse that they were experiencing.

Taking charge of one's finances is crucial to effective financial management. Most young adults are beleaguered by a myriad of problems that hamper their ability to control their finances. This usually leads to poor financial decisions that keep them perpetually tethered to a cycle of debt and impedes the achievement of financial freedom. To unshackle yourself from this, it is imperative that you acquire a good understanding of the mishaps that prevent you from developing healthy and sustainable financial behaviors and practices. Let us now look at some of the common problems and scenarios that may be getting in your way as you try to achieve financial independence.

Running Out of Money before Next Payday

According to a survey by the financial services company, Salary Finance Limited, more than a third of American workers run out of money before their next paycheck. In the report titled *Inside the Wallets of Working Americans*, 42 percent of American employees cited financial problems as the leading cause of stress. Moreover, workers who earn lower incomes are the most adversely affected by financial-related stress, with 50 percent of employees earning less than $15,000 citing financial problems as the main stress factor in their lives.

It was also found that 49 percent of workers earning between $15,000 and $25,000 experience finance-related stress. This is not very surprising, considering the rising cost of living and stagnating salaries, which make it difficult for low-income earners to have disposable income. One of the biggest factors contributing to financial stress is running out of money before the next paycheck, which happens to over 32 percent of workers, according to findings by Salary Finance.

Very often in the course of my life, I am approached by people who complain that they simply don't understand why their paycheck runs out so fast. This creates a precarious financial situation because it makes it difficult to save money for emergencies. This has become especially apparent in light of the coronavirus pandemic, which has led to massive job losses, leaving many workers in America and around the world in dire financial straits. In a survey conducted by Pew

Research Center in April 2020, only 47 percent of respondents said they have enough emergency funds to cover three months of expenses. This means that a large number of workers will need to take up more debt to cover most of their expenses. While most Americans were already living paycheck to paycheck even before the coronavirus, the emergence of this new health crisis and its attendant economic implications means that the financial security of most workers is now in jeopardy.

This is not a problem that is purely experienced by low-income earners. Even professionals who earn a quite reasonable salary usually admit that they don't know where their paycheck went. While there are myriads of reasons why most people's wages seem to disappear into thin air as soon as they are paid. I have found that poor budgeting skills are often the root cause of this. Specifically, misunderstanding how much is available as free funds after making debt, loan, mortgage, or rent payments.

Individuals who fail to budget for their paycheck in advance usually end up misallocating their finances and incurring unplanned expenses, which cause their money to run out faster. Therefore, learning how to budget appropriately and sticking to one's budget can help to mitigate this problem through planned spending.

Not Knowing the Size of Overdraft or Debt

Another common problem that hinders most people from achieving financial freedom is the failure to keep track of debt, which is due to the fact that debt and credit distort our sense of spending.

A little while ago, my sister-in-law tragically passed away from a stroke at a relatively young age. A while before, her mother passed away, and she and her sister were the beneficiaries of a decent-sized estate. The family had always lived a seemingly modest existence commensurate with modest salaries. We would be the beneficiaries of hand-me-down clothes from my nephew, of which were always plenty, of good quality brands, but we thought nothing of it. After her mother's death, they splashed a bit of money on new cars and a truck but nothing very excessive.

However, after her untimely death, not only was there no sign of the inheritance, but there were unpaid credit cards and loans. Even the house had been re-mortgaged for an increased amount, through the bank she worked at, and without the husband's knowledge. There was nothing to show for all this spending except a few wardrobes full of clothes. Even her son's inheritance from his grandma had gone. We subsequently surmised that she had been running and juggling massive debts for years, and the interest had been piling up and piling up. When she came into money, it was all swallowed up, clearing up the debts. This illustrates the negative snowball effects of debt interest once allowed to reach a critical mass they can ruin your finances forever.

If you live on a cash basis, it is psychologically easier to keep track of spending because when you hand over cash during a purchase, you don't get it back. In other words, something physical leaves your possession in exchange for the goods or services. On the other hand, when you charge your credit card, it is handed back to you. It is easy to assume that you have more funds than you do. This can lead to a ballooning of debt, which may put a lot of strain on your finances. It is therefore important to develop an awareness of your debt to prevent it from spiraling out of control. There are several warning signs that can help you to pick up on a personal debt crisis. These include:

i) Minimum Payments

While making minimum payments may afford you more flexibility when it comes to servicing your debt, it can also be detrimental to your financial stability. This is because minimum payments keep you in debt for longer. By only 'chipping' on your debt, you may get stuck on a perpetual cycle of making monthly debt payments, while interest continues to pile up. Credit card debt, for example, is easy to rack up since you may end up ignoring it as long as you are making minimum payments now and then. As a result, you will end up paying a relatively small debt for a very long time, with most of the payments going on interest, which will make it more difficult to achieve financial freedom.

ii) Struggles with Debt Collectors

If you have debt collectors or creditors constantly hounding and threatening you with repossession of property or wage garnishments, chances are you are not managing your debt properly. You need to evaluate the debt that you have racked up and begin making payments to ease your debt and prevent creditors from making these threats. Disagreements with your creditors are also telltale signs that you need to change your approach and behavior.

iii) Inability to Secure Loans or Credit Cards

Having unmanaged debt can greatly hamper your ability to secure loans from creditors. If you find that you are unable to get loans or credit on favorable terms, it means that your creditworthiness has dwindled. Creditors have little confidence in your ability to repay loans.

iv) Inability to Grow Your Savings

If you find that you have no money to put into savings after covering your bills, there is a strong likelihood that you have a debt problem. You should carefully evaluate whether your savings are increasing or decreasing since this will provide you with clues on how well you are managing your debt. If you notice that you often have to dig into your savings or retirement funds to cover your day-to-day expenses, this is a sign that you have unsustainable debt.

Impulsive or compulsive Spending - You see, you want it now!

Impulsive spending is undoubtedly a common phenomenon in today's culture of high consumption. Nearly everyone can admit to having purchased a product or service at some point simply because they thought it was attractive. The rise of online stores has made it a lot easier and convenient to shop for products and services without even having to leave the house. However, the convenience that online shopping provides has also made us more prone to spend money on things that we may not necessarily need. According to a recent survey by finder.com on consumer habits, 88.6 percent of Americans admit to having engaged in impulsive shopping online, with each individual spending an average of $81.75 per session.

While impulsive buying is not necessarily a bad thing when done occasionally, it can lead to serious problems when done regularly. Individuals who engage in frequent impulsive buying tend to overspend, and this can lead to negative feelings of guilt and self-loathing - which can give rise to a cycle of more spending to assuage these feelings.

For some people, these problems develop further and become compulsive, a habit that is out of their control; an addiction. This makes compulsive spenders prone to anxiety, low self-esteem, and unhappiness.

"I believed at the time ... that everyone had credit cards and always bought what they wanted. That is what I did. I spent a lot of time window shopping, store shopping, and buying now but paying later. I always thought I would have the money, so I lived with this heavy feeling from debt and also from living in a fantasy world. I bought things because I thought that was where happiness was." R from Spenders Anonymous.

So, why do a lot of people engage in impulse buying, given how problematic it can be? Well, here are a number of factors that may motivate individuals to spend impulsively.

i) The Desire to Save Money

Most times, when people engage in impulsive buying, the motive is usually to take advantage of the attractive discounts that are offered on items that are on sale. For instance, you may find that your favorite store has shoes on sale and think it's best to buy a pair or two. This may seem like a prudent financial decision, especially if your shoes are starting to wear out and you were already planning to buy new ones in a month or two. However, despite your very reasonable rationalization, you will still end up spending money that you did not budget. Since you hadn't factored new shoes in your budget, the reality is that you don't have the money to spend on the purchase of shoes. But your desire to save cash causes you to overlook this factor and buy them anyway.

ii) A Need to Feel Good

In the consumerist society that we live in today, there is pressure for people to purchase things they don't need to compensate for any insecurities or dissatisfactions that they experience. Companies are constantly conducting aggressive advertising campaigns that are designed to make people believe that they would be happier, more attractive, or successful if they purchase their products. As a result, individuals feel pressured into spending a lot of money on things that don't add tangible value to their lives.

When I was younger, my wife and I visited a couple - the husband worked at the same firm as my wife. While we were at their house, I was staggered by the rows and rows of VHS cassettes, hundreds of them. Box set, after box set, after box set. There on the wall were several thousand worths of spending, and this was a young couple with a new mortgage. I couldn't believe anyone could pour so much money into buying stuff they had *(probably)* already watched on television or at the cinema. Furthermore, DVDs were just coming in, so they were all about to be rendered obsolete. They split up with massive debts, and he was left paying off the cost of those box sets for years afterwards.

iii) Made up lists of wants

There is a natural tendency to see things, and then to want them. We are surrounded by programs, films, social media, and advertisements that are designed to produce 'desire' for a lifestyle or physical items. We start to add things to an imaginary list of wants that we then fulfill. Even when it is not as extreme as the case of Kirk, below, it is mentally damaging as it leads to low-level unhappiness and dissatisfaction.

"My compulsive spending problem is intricately linked with my Obsessive-Compulsive Disorder (OCD). I make lists of things to do and buy. When I get going on a list, it can be like an avalanche of activity. Not only will I try to finish buying every-

thing on the list, but inevitably I will end up buying many other things that were not on the list. I have run up credit card bills that I didn't know how I would pay off. I recognize when I am engaged in a spending spree, but I often have felt powerless to stop myself. The compulsion to finish the list and to avoid adding other things to the list - by buying them right then - has often been much stronger than the recognition that I didn't have the money to pay for what I was buying." Kirk from Spenders Anonymous

Paying off Debt that Eats a Huge Chunk of Your Income

While regular payments to creditors can manage small debts, larger debts are usually a lot harder to control. If you allow your debt to spiral out of hand, you may end up in a scenario whereby you are making sizable debt payments, which can carve out a huge percentage of your earnings.

Taking on debt is essentially the same as spending future income. The money that you earn in the future is spent on repaying the principal as well as the accumulated interest. Many people take on debt in an expectation that their future income will rise; this assumption can often fail to materialize. If you don't manage your debt early, it may eventually get to a point where all your income that is not used in necessities ends up servicing the interest on your debt. When it gets to this point, this is where the house of cards collapses.

The following table illustrates the amount of interest you will pay on some example loans. Remember that interest is the amount of your future income that you will be handing over for the privilege of consuming something today rather than delaying it. You should convert the amount of interest you will pay into the number of hours you would have to work to earn the equivalent amount. This gives you a sense of the real cost of your spending and debt.

Table 1 The Real Cost of Debt

	Mortgage	**Vehicle Loan**	**Credit Card**	**Pay Day**
Amount Borrowed (Principal)	$300,000	$30,000	$3,000	$300
Simple Interest Rate	4.7% Annual	8.64% Annual	25.6% Annual	20% for 14 Days
APR (Exclusive Fees)	5.0%	9.0%	29%	521%
Term of Loan	30 Years	3 Years	Revolving	14 Days
Interest to be Paid	$996,582	$8,467	$870	$1,563
Total Amount Owed	$1,296,582	$38,467	$3,870	$1,863

All loans are assumed to have monthly compounding *(when interest is paid on unpaid interest)*, except for payday loans, which are fortnightly (14 days).

Interest to be paid assumes you make no payments over the term. In the case of the credit card, we have used one year.

All fees and charges are excluded. The fees for non-payment, or making new loan arrangements are usually exorbitant, especially for payday loans, and could easily double the actual APR. Credit card companies may also charge a higher (penalty) rate following non-payment.

APR = Annualised percentage rate. This is simple interest expressed in a way that makes a comparison valid for different compounding periods, the same way we use miles *per hour* to compare speed.

YOLO Lifestyle

Many millennials today have embraced a YOLO lifestyle, living in the moment, with instant gratification, without worrying too much about the future. Let's face it, the future seems very far away when you are twenty-something. One of the serious dangers of the YOLO mentality is that it promotes overspending. Individuals who subscribe to this philosophy are likely to justify purchasing things they cannot afford by incurring debt. It shouldn't come as a surprise then, that the overwhelming majority of individuals who profess this kind of lifestyle are broke most of the time.

As harmless as it may seem at face value, however, the YOLO-style of spending can be very detrimental to one's long term financial stability. Failing to manage immediate financial concerns properly can lead to perpetual financial stress and make it impossible to achieve any kind of prosperity and financial calm.

Overlooking the importance of financially responsible behaviors such as saving and budgeting, may seem inconsequential now, but takes on a different perspective once you arrive in your forties with half your working life behind you and nothing to show, but a pile of debt and a nice Instagram feed.

Never have money, so when you get it you just spend it

Managing money is a habit, which means that when you finally get some, it can slip through your fingers like water. If you don't have a regular source of income, you are more likely to have a pile-up of expenses, and as a result, end up spending all your money as soon as you earn it. This is what makes it difficult for you to develop a habit of saving and growing your disposable income, thus keeping you in a loop of debt and borrowing. Furthermore, having an unstable income makes it slightly more complex to manage your finances and plan for the future, we will address the solution to this later.

Looking for "Get Rich Quick" solutions

The world today is saturated with countless scam enterprises that offer unsuspecting victims overinflated promises of fortune that turn out to be fraudulent. Mainstream culture, and governments, have to a great extent, abetted this get-rich-quick mindset through media portrayals of ordinary folks winning astronomical sums of money in lotteries, gaming platforms, and pyramid schemes. As a result, some people believe that using a lottery win will fund their retirement. Of course, the economics of lotteries makes this wholly implausible. The allure of easy money can drive you on a dangerous path of financial and emotional ruin, not to mention wastage of time, energy, and resources, which could have been channeled to better use.

There are several reasons why get-rich schemes simply do not work, and will not help you to make a fortune as some marketers of these enterprises would like you to believe. These include:

i) They do not Obey the Law of Equity

In every aspect of life, there is a direct correlation between the amount of input that is given and the output that results from it. If you work out physically in the gym, for instance, you can build muscle and cut down on your weight, thereby becoming more healthy. Likewise, if you spend a lot of time and effort trying to learn and perfect a particular skill, you develop mastery in that field. As a result, you will be able to execute your tasks perfectly and with ease.

The same thing is true when it comes to building wealth

and fortune. To obtain wealth and be able to manage it properly, you need to invest a lot of time, money, patience, and effort. This allows you to develop the know-how of wealth-creation and management, which will enable you to sustain your fortune. On the other hand, if you acquire wealth without putting in the commensurate effort, you may not have the experience that is required to sustain it.

ii) Easily Acquired Wealth Often Disappears just as Quickly

Majority of people who suddenly become wealthy due to windfalls such as winning the lottery often end up going broke in a few months or years. The reason for this is that people who suddenly acquire wealth without making an effort tend not to value it enough. As a result, they may dish out large sums of money to their family and friends, spend extravagantly on vanity projects and liability goods, and fail to monitor their spending.

iii) Get Rich Schemes are Prone to False Advertising

Most enterprises that promise quick riches often deliberately misrepresent their schemes to take advantage of the desperation of unsuspecting individuals. They may, for instance, advertise themselves as legitimate investment opportunities while offering no tangible benefits or affiliate marketing scams that promise people large sums of income for doing menial tasks. In some cases, they may even be 'rich relative' scams which trick their victims into thinking they have won a windfall from a wealthy relation. Instead, these enterprises simply prey on unsuspecting individuals and swindle them of their money.

Although there is nothing inherently evil about wanting

to get as far as possible with minimal effort, resorting to these get-rich-quick schemes can make you an easy target for would-be scammers who are only looking to leave your pockets dry. The major issues with these schemes are that they divert us into wasting time, energy, and money, and derail us from the real path to prosperity. So, the first step in building healthy financial behavior is to understand that nothing comes easy, and you will have to put in some tangible effort to reap the rewards that you are seeking. Once you become aware of this fact, you will develop an appreciation of 'financial discipline' and begin to work on managing your finances more effectively.

In summary, here are the main takeaways from this chapter:

- Achieving financial freedom requires you to understand the problems and issues that have delivered you here at this moment in time.
- Get -rich -quick schemes are not effective ways of creating wealth. Expect to get out what you put in.
- Make a list for yourself of all the financial problems that you have in your life, and for each problem to identify the root cause of that problem. This will come in handy later.

CHAPTER TWO: UNDERSTAND YOUR BEHAVIOR AND HOW IT IS MANIPULATED

In this chapter, we shall examine and attempt to understand the causes of problem behavior and how it impacts your finances. We will look at how marketers are manipulating your normal human responses and how you can resist these cynical ploys.

You will learn about the:

- 5 common problems sabotaging your prosperity
- 7 debt myths that are keeping you impoverished
- The difference between good debt and bad debt
- 5 Psychological Weapons being used to make you overspend
- How to protect yourself from influencers

Becoming financially responsible is one of the most important aspects of being an adult. If you've recently left home and are trying to chart your path in the world, it is vital that you learn how to manage your finances properly to sustain your lifestyle and grow your wealth. Nevertheless, there are many habits that we often pick along the way, which may make it harder to achieve financial freedom. If you find that you tend to be broke most of the time despite having a source of income, here are some of the areas you may be going wrong.

5 common Problems Sabotaging your Prosperity

i) You Lack the Right Mindset

Having the right mindset is crucial when it comes to developing behaviors that will help you to achieve financial success. This is simply because your thoughts will tend to translate into actions. So, before you even embark on the task of effecting financial discipline in your life, you need first to make a conscious decision that you want to create wealth and achieve financial freedom. Once you convince yourself that you are capable of becoming wealthy and make the choice to work towards that goal, you will have the motivation and drive to implement the necessary changes in your behavior and lifestyle.

ii) Failure to Budget

In order to plan your financial life in a sustainable way, you must learn how to budget your money. Having a budget not only allows you to keep your expenses low but also enables you to make shrewd investments.

By cutting down on your expenses, you will be able to save money, which you can deposit in an emergency fund account to keep you financially secure in case unplanned or unexpected events arise.

iii) Overspending

One of the negative outcomes of failing to budget is that you end up spending more than you earn. This can make it difficult to save money or even have spare funds to channel into wealth-generating assets. Furthermore, overspending also increases the likelihood of excessive borrowing, which can cause you to rake in a lot of debt to fund unaffordable consumption.

iv) Failing to Invest

Unless you are the top 'C' levels of a large company, the chances of becoming rich from your salary are very low. To generate real wealth, you need to invest your income in projects that have the potential for high returns. In other words, you need to make your money work for you instead of working for money.

iv) Failing to Prioritize Debt Repayment

One of the common financial mistakes that people often make is to put off paying debt or only paying minimal amounts. This can be very counterproductive since it prolongs the period of repayment *(which can result in paying higher interest rates).*

So, to achieve financial freedom, you need to take an aggressive stance when it comes to clearing your debt. By making debt clearance a top priority, you will be able to pull yourself out of the vicious debt cycle a lot faster, and eventually have spare cash to redirect to wealth-generating opportunities. We will discuss different approaches to clearing this debt later in the book.

v) Fear of Failure

Many people often get stuck in poor financial situations simply because they are afraid of failing. They may worry that financial management is a complicated and time-consuming process, for which they are just not cut out. They may also lack confidence in their ability to make good decisions and wrongly assume they will end up making mistakes. If fear is the only thing holding you back from reaching for financial success, you need to understand that failure is a part of life, and your mistakes help you to learn. After all, it is impossible to succeed in anything without making an effort to try.

7 Debt Myths that are keeping you impoverished

Having affordable debt is not necessarily a bad thing, but is generally counterproductive except as we will discuss. Most businesses grow and develop as a result of loans acquired from lending institutions such as banks. They do this by using it to generate a higher return than the cost of the debt. However, when you manage debt poorly, it can quickly become a serious financial problem, which can lead to brokenness. Therefore, understanding how debt works and how you can control it is very crucial when it comes to managing your finances properly.

There are several wrong beliefs about debt that most people tend to hold, which affect their finances and decision-making strategies. Let us now look at some of these common myths, and see whether there is any truth to them.

Myth 1: Debt is either good or bad

According to a survey conducted by PricewaterhouseCoopers in 2017, debt is one of the main causes of financial stress for American workers. This is not entirely surprising, because the average American household owes a total debt of $134,643. Nevertheless, rising debt levels and the strain that they exert on individual incomes have created the general perception that debt is always a bad thing. However, some types of debt can lead to better financial outcomes, thus enabling one to improve their future wealth prospects.

In general, any kind of debt that is channeled towards investments *(which can potentially increase your income)* or used to purchase an appreciating asset you can consider as good debt. Let's look at some examples to understand the difference between good and bad debt.

a. Mortgages

Most workers are not able to purchase homes in cash due to insufficient income and day-to-day expenses, which take up most of their paychecks. For this reason, many homebuyers typically end up having to take on some debt in the form of mortgages to buy a property. This can be advantageous because it allows individuals with good credit scores to receive loans at reasonable interests to invest in a home, which has historically been an appreciating asset. However, a mortgage can very easily become a bad debt if you overextend yourself purchasing a property that leaves insufficient free income to meet your other needs, or even if it just drains your cashflow such that you cannot make proper provision for investing and retirement. Failure to maintain the payments can lead to foreclosures and repossession of the property by your lender.

b. Vehicle Loans

Taking up debt to procure a vehicle *(which is beyond your means)* is undoubtedly a bad idea, even though low finance rates appear to make it more palatable. This is especially true because there are other payments to be made, for instance, insurance and maintenance. Cars are fast depreciating assets, and the amount of your loan can easily exceed the value.

Various types of finance deals are available on vehicles, which makes them superficially attractive. For example, a personal contract plan (PCP) that requires a minimum deposit, and at the end of the contract, you are required to make a final (balloon) payment or hand the vehicle back. A PCP is designed to keep you coming back every three years for a new vehicle, even though the lifespan of a car is now many times that. The average price of new cars and the level of equipment has been rising steadily since these schemes became widespread because the 'reasonable' monthly cost hides the real cost. Adopting these financing plans could drain your cashflow in interest payments, which you could otherwise invest in other projects.

Car payments could be taking up the second largest part of your post tax income after mortgage or rent payments. However they are much more easily controlled by making trade-offs.

c. Student Loans

Student loans are, without a doubt, one of the most common debts that many people take up in the course of their lives. However, with millions of borrowers defaulting on these loans every year, it can be difficult to perceive this kind of debt as good. The truth of the matter is that student loans can be good or bad, depending on how you leverage them. For instance, if you borrow a small amount to pay for a course in a reasonably priced college or university, this can be considered as a reasonably good loan, given that your earnings are likely to increase once you attain higher education.

On the other hand, taking up too much debt to finance a college or university education in an expensive institution can be a liability in the event that you fail to secure a high-paying career. If you are thinking about securing a loan to pay for college, therefore, you need to choose an institution and loan amount, aligned with your potential future earnings.

As a rule of thumb, good debt is one that promises future benefits, either in terms of increased earnings or improved quality of life. In contrast, bad debt is one that is likely to cost you more money in the future or leave you worse off than if you hadn't taken the debt in the first place.

Any kind of debt that you incur as a result of financing a lifestyle that is beyond your earnings you should consider as a bad debt. For instance, if you charge your credit card to pay for things like fancy clothes, entertainment, and expensive phones, then carry forward the debt every month. You will eventually end up accruing more interest, which may sink you into debt even further. Conversely, if you borrow some money from a bank to set up a side hustle to supplement your income, you will be able to repay the loan from the profits that your enterprise generates, thus improving your financial prospects.

Myth 2: You Should Only Start to Save Once You Have Finished Paying Your Debt

Many people often wrongly believe that they should save once an individual has completely cleared all their outstanding debt. While this may seem rather logical at face value, channeling all your spare income to debt repayments may not be the ideal way to go, especially if you have large outstanding debts. It is therefore advisable to approach your financial situation from a balanced perspective; we will discuss this later in the book.

Myth 3: You Will Lose Your Possessions if You Fail to Repay Your Outstanding Debt

It is not uncommon for people to worry that creditors will repossess their possessions if they are declared bankrupt. This, however, should not be a reason for concern. While lenders can repossess homes and vehicles in case owners are unable to repay the debt, personal effects, household goods, and furniture are generally exempt from bankruptcy claims. Nevertheless, there are instances where your creditors may ask you to include items of high value *(such as expensive paintings and luxury cars)* in a sworn Statement of Affairs. As long as you make regular payments to your creditors, you are likely to keep all your possessions.

Myth 4: You Will Lose Your Job if You are Unable to Payback Your Debt

Many people often express concern about getting fired by their employers if they file for bankruptcy. The truth of the matter, however, is that it is illegal for employers to dismiss their employees from the workplace, simply because they have defaulted on their debt payments or filed a bankruptcy claim. Your employer will not even be informed about your bankruptcy unless there is a wage garnishment order. In case this order is granted *(by a court),* your employer may be tasked to withhold a certain amount of your paycheck and send it directly to your creditor until the debt has been cleared.

Myth 5: You will be Unable to Secure Credit in Future if You Declare Bankruptcy

While most people tend to perceive bankruptcy as some kind of punishment for loan defaulters, it is designed to be rehabilitative. It would, therefore, be unfair for individuals to be punished for the rest of their lives simply for failing to meet their loan obligations. In general, people who declare bankruptcy are listed on credit reports for a maximum of 6 years before they are dropped off. This essentially means that you can still secure loans and mortgages from lenders in the future, once you are discharged from bankruptcy.

Myth 6: Bankruptcy is the Only Option if You have Large Outstanding Debt

While most people often see bankruptcy as the only solution for large debt, there are several measures that you can take to solve a debt problem without having to declare bankruptcy. Bankruptcy should only be considered as a final resort after all other options have been exhausted. One of the main ways in which you can solve a debt problem is through debt management. In this approach, multiple loans are combined into a single loan to lower the interest and make payment a lot easier. Another option that you can consider to deal with large outstanding debts is a settlement. This involves negotiating with your creditors to have a part of your debt erased. As a result, the outstanding debt is reduced, thereby easing the pressure of repayment.

Myth 7: Late Credit-Card Payments will Hurt Your Credit Rating

Granted, late credit-card payments are far from ideal.

This is because they lead to the accumulation of fees and increase interest charges. However, just because you are late on your payment doesn't mean your credit score will be affected. In general, companies do not report credit card payments unless they are overdue by more than 30 days. So you have no reason to worry about getting listed on credit bureaus as long as you make the payment within the month.

Managing 'Bad Spending' Behaviors

We live in an increasingly materialistic world that promotes compulsive spending and buying things that we often don't need. Every single day we are bombarded with advertisements which tell us we won't be happy unless we acquire the latest trendy gadget or product that is on sale. It is no surprise then that most people run out of money as soon as they receive their paycheck and end up racking huge debts in a bid to furnish their expensive lifestyles.

Compulsive spending is one of the most common addictions in today's society. Unfortunately, most people don't consider it an addiction problem because no physical symptoms are involved. Nevertheless, compulsive spending can be a serious addiction issue not very different from other addictions such as drugs, sex, and gambling.

First, people usually engage in impulse buying to feel good about themselves and avoid negative feelings such as anxiety and depression. Compulsive spending is often rooted in feelings of inadequacy and low self-esteem but can be exacerbated by mood disorders. Many believe that by buying all the fancy and expensive things that are marketed by companies, they will be able to fill the void in their lives and achieve happiness. Sure, charging your credit card, or any spending, can give you a temporary feeling of power and freedom. However, the more you continue to overspend in things you do not need, funding an unsustainable lifecycle, ultimately fuels the cycle of self-loathing, anxiety, and depression.

Just as with other pleasurable activities such as sex and drug use, spending typically activates reward centers in the brain and stimulates the release of the 'feel-good' hormone dopamine. The more you spend money to trigger this good feeling, the higher the surge of dopamine. As a result, you end up getting caught up in a cycle of overspending on things that you don't need to chase that dopamine high. The happy feeling that one experiences due to compulsive spending can provide temporary relief from negative feelings such as anxiety and stress. However, when the spending becomes too much, it often results in high debts, which can further exacerbate one's mental problems and disrupt their lives.

If you want to achieve financial success and freedom, therefore, you need to overcome your bad spending habits and develop good behaviors when it comes to how you manage your money. To do so, it is important to be able to identify the symptoms of compulsive spending addiction. Here are some of the telltale signs that can help you to diagnose this problem:

- Spending a significant amount of your income in arbitrary and unplanned purchases
- Accumulating a large amount of consumer debt
- Inability to stop spending despite having a desire to do so
- Hiding purchase items from close relatives and friends
- Being more excited about purchasing things than actually owning them
- Purchasing items which you end up not using

- Buying a large number of products which you do not need
- Having relationship problems due to bad spending habits
- Experiencing negative feelings such as shame and guilt from your spending habits
- Feeling excited or uneasy when shopping
- Using spending as a coping mechanism to deal with unpleasant emotions such as low self-esteem, anxiety, and depression.

Unlike most addictions, compulsive spending disorder can be very challenging to quit, especially if you have spare income most of the time. Nevertheless, cognitive behavioral therapy can help to mitigate this problem by addressing the psychological factors which contribute to needless spending. Overcoming the challenge of compulsive spending also requires a total change in one's mindset.

Desire: Are You Being Manipulated Into Spending More?

It is hard to go through your day without coming across numerous ads whether on TV, social media, or billboards, seeking to draw your attention to all kinds of products in the hope of convincing you to buy whatever it is they are marketing. While there is nothing inherently wrong with advertising, many companies today employ manipulative tactics, which are psychologically influencing us into spending money on things that we don't need. These techniques are so effective, relying on our social conditioning, that we will not realize that they manipulated us.

In contemporary times, ads have become far more complex and nuanced, often employing eye-catching visuals, sophisticated graphics, and carefully choreographed stories, which create lasting impressions about the products. The memories that this creates on the mind of consumers through ads can have a profound emotional impact on them and influence their decision on whether or not to buy a certain product.

One of the fundamental things to realize about mass consumer advertising is that it doesn't care if you can afford the product, as long as you buy it. Marketeers deliberately want you to aspire to their product so they can increase the profit margins. By purchasing the product, you believe that you take on the desirable characters and traits of the people using the product in the advertising. In essence, ads raise the desire for a product so that you *perceive* the value to be in excess of the cost.

If you are struggling with everyday expenses and bills, you probably don't have a lot of money to spare for purchasing the latest expensive phone or other luxury items. But since ads are *always* designed to appeal to your emotions, you may find yourself taking on debt simply to own a fancy product that is marketed at you, which will ultimately mess with your budget and lead to money problems.

Advertisements are designed to arouse extrinsic motivation to influence you to purchase things that may not necessarily be useful to you. Intrinsically motivated people usually have an innate feeling of self-acceptance and will do things because they intuitively believe they are good for them. On the other hand, extrinsically motivated people tend to focus too much on how others perceive them and are more likely to prioritize social acceptance and popularity than personal happiness and fulfillment. Advertisers are very conscious of this fact, which is why they employ messaging tactics to evoke desire in consumers and make them believe that they won't be whole, happy, or accepted unless they own a particular product.

Desire is a very powerful emotion that can overrun one's ability to make rational decisions. Therefore, before purchasing any product that is being advertised, you should take the time to think it through carefully to ascertain whether you are buying it because you need it, or simply because the advertisers tell you that you do. One useful tactic that you can employ is to enforce a mandatory holding strategy on your spending, whereby you wait 72 hours before deciding to purchase a product. This will give you enough time to decide whether you want to proceed with the transaction or not.

One of the factors that usually drives people to spend is the perception that whatever they own is not enough. For instance, you may feel like your possessions, such as your phone, car, or house, are not as good as someone else's. This can lead to feelings of inadequacy, which consequently push you to spend more to try to attain the same status. It is important to realize that every individual's circumstances are unique, and so comparing yourself with them (especially fictitious advertising characters) serves no useful purpose other than to dent your self-esteem and confidence. By avoiding the stimuli - which gives you a false perception - you can develop a healthy sense of being and completeness, thus eliminating buying things that you don't really need.

5 Psychological Weapons used to make you overspend

We have talked in general about the power of advertising to change our behavior. Now we are going to learn about 5 specific methods or tricks that are used every day to influence us and increase our desire for materialistic things.

Contrast principle

When we experience similar things in succession or simultaneously, we evaluate the lesser or greater value of the second through direct comparison with the first.

This contrast effect will create an increased or diminished perception of the second thing dependent on how we viewed the first. For example, when you lift a heavy bag and then a lighter one, the second bag will appear lighter than it really is. This contrast effect is because our brain evaluates things based on the comparison that is most easily accessible at that given moment, rather than the most suitable one. Thus, we evaluate by reference to convenient comparisons rather than by using absolute values, which are more correct, as these aren't readily available for our brains to utilize - *this often leads us to make biassed judgments.*

The contrast effect applies to many judgments we make day-to-day. For example, if at a cocktail party, you talk to an unattractive person, and are then joined by an average-looking person, you will judge the average-looking person to be more attractive than they really are. Also, more so than you would have perceived them to be, had you seen them on their own, before you had this unreliable scale of comparison implanted. In this way, the Contrast effect can affect our judgments concerning people, products, market values, and the values of many other attributes and characteristics.

The contrast principle has many applications in sales and marketing and is often utilized by brands to influence customers' perceptions of their products. For example, a technique commonly used by salespeople is to offer either low quality or an overpriced luxury item, alongside the one they really want you to buy. They do this to influence your perception of this target product as being a good value deal in comparison to the other items they offered.

Reciprocity

People are socially obliged to give back to others the form of a behavior, gift, or service that they have received first.

If a friend invites you to their party, you feel obligated to ask them to a future party you are hosting. If a colleague does you a favor, then you owe that colleague a favor. In the context of a social obligation, people are more likely to say yes to those who they owe.

This principle is exploited ruthlessly. Charities know this well, which is why they send a free gift, such as a pen when they are soliciting donations. Likewise, restaurants exploit this when they give you a mint along with your bill. This simple act will increase tips by 3%.

Authority

'Authority' is the idea that people follow the lead of credible, knowledgeable experts. Physiotherapists, for example, can persuade more of their patients to comply with recommended exercise programs if they display their medical diplomas on the walls of their consulting rooms. People are more likely to give change for a parking meter to a stranger if that requester wears a uniform rather than casual clothes.

What the science is telling us is that it's important to signal to others what makes you a credible, knowledgeable authority before you make your influence attempt.

In the same vein, advertisers will use authority figures like dentists to market their products, such as toothpaste or toothbrushes, as the claims appear more credible.

Scarcity

People always want more of those things they can have less of. For instance, when British Airways announced in 2003 that they would no longer be operating the twice-daily

London to New York Concorde flight because it had become uneconomical to run, sales took-off (pun intended) the very next day.

Notice that nothing had changed about Concorde itself. It didn't fly any faster, the service didn't suddenly get better, and the airfare didn't drop. It had simply become a scarce resource. And as a result, people wanted it more.

This is why sales are always ending today, or for one day only. They want you to believe that you will miss out if you don't grab that bargain right now.

Consistency

Consistency is an adaptive behavior that has been very beneficial. Doing certain things always in the same way and making decisions according to the same values help us survive in a complex world.

We feel bad if we say we are going to do one thing and then we don't do it. We unconsciously strive for consistency in our commitments. We prefer to follow pre-existing attitudes, values, and actions, so it is much more likely that we end up doing something after having admitted to agreeing with it – verbally or in writing. Not only do we want to "be" consistent, but we also need to "look" consistent.

The more effort you put into doing something, the more influential the Principle of Consistency will be.

In Cialdini's research, he found that not only will people go out of their way to behave consistently, they will also feel positive about being consistent with their decisions, even when faced with evidence that their decisions were erroneous.

For example, at the racetracks, people are much more confident of their horse's chances of winning just after placing the bet than they are immediately before laying down that bet.

Second, we don't know ourselves that well. Sometimes, we say something or do something without thinking it through beforehand. Then our mind says: "OK, I just bought my third Starbucks in a week. I must really like coffee and Starbucks. Maybe, I even can't function properly without them." It's similar to forcing yourself to smile when feeling sad. It makes you less sad because your brain gets the information on your mood from the physiological action you made.

Third, sometimes we'll decide on our identity and hence our behavior by looking at what others think about us. Housewives from New Haven, Connecticut, gave much more money to a charity after hearing that they were considered charitable people.

Such automatic decision-making plus the stubbornness to stick with this decision is a gift to anyone who'd want to influence your behavior for better or worse

Poverty is not relative - we just perceive it that way

The rise of social media platforms in the past two decades has undoubtedly revolutionized the way we interact with each other. Sites such as Facebook, Instagram, and Twitter, constantly keep us in touch with our friends, family, and acquaintances and peek into their lives without being constrained by the barriers of distance or time. While this increased connectedness has produced a transformational effect on our personal relationships, it has also come at considerable cost to our mental health and the way we perceive ourselves.

Picture this. You are scrolling through your newsfeeds on Facebook or Instagram and suddenly, an image of one of your friends having a great time at a posh restaurant pops up on your screen. They seem to be happy and smiling, which makes you envious of them. Immediately you begin to think about your meager income and the fact that you're not able to afford a meal at such a swish location. This will likely cause you to feel inadequate and inferior, thus feeding into the negative thoughts you often have about yourself. Your self-esteem ends up taking a hit, and your self-confidence diminishes. A friend said to me, you are always out and about eating in nice places. As my wife will attest, that is inaccurate, but this is because the only time I post on social media is when we go out! After all, the rest of our life is as mundane as the next person. What he was seeing from his Facebook feed was a complete caricature of our lives.

People tend to portray themselves on social media in choreographed ways to appeal to other users. There is a lot of pressure on social media for people to present themselves in glamorous vignettes to achieve popularity and influence on these platforms, when in real life, they may be struggling like everyone else. If you take the flashy images you see on social media as accurate representations of people's real-life experiences, you are going to *feel* poor and inadequate.

It is worth remembering, *in fact,* poverty is *not* relative. Real poverty is living in a shack, without access to running water or proper sanitation, where if you don't work that day, then you won't eat. Billions of people live that type of existence.

So, although you may *feel* poor as compared to some of your friends or acquaintances in social media, there is always someone else who is worse off than you. By appreciating yourself and what you have going for you at the moment, you can eliminate the tendency of comparing yourself with others and the need to show off on social media.

How to Arm yourself against manipulation

There are a number of steps that we can take to fight back against the barrage of advertising, social media and other negative influences.

- Realize that your self worth is not a function of your possessions or even wealth, and work on reinforcing that.
- Develop the habits and practices of internal rather than external motivation. Look to your internalized set of values for reference, not what is happening around you at the moment.
- Reduce or eliminate your exposure to social media and the news or TV
- Replace these stimuli with meaningful hobbies or past-times that give you purpose and pleasure.

I know it sounds trite, but you should spend time each day counting your blessings and looking at positive events in your life because it works to improve your mental strength.

Let us refresh some of the main points that we have picked from this chapter.

- Understanding and changing one's spending behaviors is absolutely crucial when it comes to developing good financial discipline
- Marketers and advertisers take advantage of people's weaknesses and insecurities to promote the sale and purchase of products which they do not need
- Compulsive spending can be an addiction, which can lead to financial as well as psychosocial

problems, and you should overcome it to be financially empowered.
- Comparing ourselves with others only breeds negative feelings about our own self-worth and drives us to spend copious amounts of money to feel good about ourselves.
- By practicing self-love, we can develop healthy strategies to cope with difficult emotions and eliminate the tendency of impulsive buying
- Develop the habits and behaviors of intrinsic motivation to protect yourself from negative influences.
- Make a list of all the times over the past few weeks you have compared yourself unfavorably to others, and consider the circumstances.
- Then do an exercise to look at all the positives in your life, including your relationships.
- Consider giving up social media for a week or two and see if you feel better off without it.

CHAPTER THREE: WHAT YOU NEED TO CHANGE TO ACHIEVE YOUR FINANCIAL AND LIFE GOALS

WE SPENT THE LAST CHAPTER LOOKING AT SOME OF THE behaviors and psychological aspects that could be driving your negative relationship with money. I hope that you also spent some time relating this to your own experiences and analyzing how this has impacted your personal finances. The conclusion of this introspection could be a realization that many of your financial problems are rooted in behavioral issues driven by bad habits.

To be successful in making these changes, we need to replace our habits with new ones. Of course, you don't develop good habits overnight; it will take mental awareness and vigilance over time - discipline.

This is the point where many financial self-help books will tell you that you just need will power! Self-restraint! Discipline! But the truth is, they are setting you up to fail! As we shall discover, will power is a much rarer commodity than you may believe. No, these good habits will not just develop in us; we need to build a framework on which they can climb, like a trellis that supports the vine. So, in this chapter, you will learn about:

- 5 psychological barriers that are holding you back
- Undoing root causes of these barriers & conditioned behaviors
- Why willpower is overrated
- How to build our new mental framework

For those readers who are impatient for practical things that they put into practice, I would beg just a little more indulgence. This chapter contains critical information that will change your life. The rest of the book is of a more practical nature, but that is of limited utility without the right attitude and approach. Without this framework, your vine of change is likely to collapse on the ground where your financial grapes of prosperity will molder away. *(Apologies for the fruity metaphor).*

5 Psychological Barriers that are Holding you Back from Achieving Change

Habits, by their very nature, are tough to break. Once a particular behavior has become ingrained in your brain, it becomes natural and automatic. In the right context, with the right triggers, you will find yourself engaging in the habit automatically, whenever you don't consciously think about it. The reason why habits are automatic is that they are literally burned into the neural pathways of the brain like little computer programs.

Once one of these programs starts to run in your brain, then it will execute to the end before reporting back your conscious self. This is why we can do something else with our conscious thoughts while engaging in 'habits'.

So, to break out of any habit (whether smoking, drug addiction, poor eating habits, or compulsive spending), it is important to become aware of the psychological factors that hinder you from making progress. Let us now go over a few of these barriers and see how they may impede you from effecting change in your behavior.

- Approval Seeking

While it is natural to want the validation of others, constantly seeking people's approval can hinder you from making any progress towards your goals. If you are always trying to impress others by spending money that you don't have on things that you don't need, sooner or later, you are going to run into financial problems. It is therefore good to develop self-awareness and knowledge since this will allow you to become comfortable in your uniqueness and become more accepting of yourself. Ultimately, you need to realize that you only answer to yourself.

- Shifting Blame

Very often, we tend to shift responsibility for our shortcomings and blame others to avoid coming to terms with our imperfect nature. Indeed, it can be tempting to attribute your negative addictive habits such as binge eating and drug addiction to other people or external factors. This allows you to avoid taking responsibility for your failures and dealing with the attendant negative feelings such as guilt and shame. However, while shifting blame can provide you with temporary relief and make you feel vindicated, it is ultimately ineffective when it comes to dealing with failure, and can significantly hinder you from making progress in your goals. Blaming external factors is easily the most common reason people will give for why they haven't achieved their goals. This is on you and no one else; you need to accept personal responsibility to change successfully.

However, we will look at some techniques we can use that will help us immensely.

- Low Self Esteem

Regardless of how healthy your goals are, you will not be able to achieve them unless you believe that you have what it takes to succeed. If you always doubt your ability to change bad habits, you will end up getting stuck in a loop of negative thoughts, which will hinder you from taking action. The doubts are driven by low self-esteem, identifying this root cause will help you feel confident enough to follow through with your decision to change your behavior even when challenges crop up along the way. In the next section of this chapter, we will look at the root causes of low esteem and discuss how we can reverse this.

- Procrastination

Procrastination is the habit of putting off until tomorrow what can be done today. We are especially prone to do this when a task is difficult, boring, or distasteful. To avoid facing this, we often use displacement activity, which is simply doing something else, even though the original task is more important or critical. It is important to realize that changing your bad money habits won't happen overnight. In all likelihood, you will require persistence and patience to succeed in this endeavor. You need to start today and become proactive in your approach to behavioral change. If you are trying to quit smoking or start dieting to improve your weight, it may be tempting to put off starting until after your birthday, or Christmas, or vacations, or when it calms down at work. The excuses can be endless, but they are all still excuses. Sitting around, waiting for other things to happen first will lead to failure and disappointment.

"In my experience, things don't happen to great men. They go out and make things happen around them." Leonardo Da Vinci

- Perfectionism

While there is nothing inherently wrong about wanting the best outcome in anything you do, having a perfectionist mindset can be a hindrance to progress when it comes to executing behavioral change. Continually striving to be perfect in everything you do only puts unnecessary pressure on you, which can lead to disappointment if things don't go as you had hoped. If you are trying to observe a strict diet, for instance, you may find yourself falling back on your poor eating habits once in a while. This does not mean that you are a complete failure or that you have some kind of character flaw. On the contrary, failing provides you with the opportunity to reevaluate the situation and learn how to navigate the challenges that you encounter more effectively. You should, therefore, adopt a balanced attitude and set realistic expectations for yourself when trying to get rid of unhelpful habits, including compulsive spending.

So far, we have identified some of the possible issues that may be holding you back from changing your behavior. These include low self-esteem, belief that you will always fail, fear of failure, living for today, and procrastination. Notably, many of these issues are deeply rooted in our self-image, and we must begin to dig them out to plant a fresh, new, healthier self-image.

Confronting Yourself: Who You are Now is not Who you will Be

This is a delicate topic as it goes to the root of who we believe we are. Most of our deep-rooted beliefs are developed from childhood, and out of these beliefs, our habits arise and become conditioned.

Significant but seemingly minor events in our life, especially pre-adolescence, can create a self-image that can be highly destructive. If a parent told you that you were greedy, or bad with money, these things could become rooted deep in your self-image, which will then feed directly into your actions because of the need to live up your self-image.

A plastic surgeon and author called Max Maltz wrote an authoritative and famous book on self-image. He observed that when performing plastic surgery on a person's face, it could completely transform their character, even their abilities. However, he also noticed that sometimes it did not. After undergoing surgery, the person still felt they were ugly and unworthy, that changing their appearance had no impact on their self-image. He concluded that in the former case, the person's self-image had been changed, but not in the latter. Furthermore, he observed that the nature of a persons' self-image was highly determinant of their success in life.

For example, you may believe that you are bad at maths (perhaps you failed a test or failed to grasp some mathematical theory). Since that belief is now rooted in your self-image, you may 'freeze' and be unable to focus your brain when you are confronted publicly with some easy mental arithmetic. The problem is that a (single) failure has been allowed to take root, which then becomes self-repeating and self-fulfilling through our automatic behaviors.

"This self-image becomes a golden key to living a better life because of two important discoveries. 1. All your actions, feelings, behaviors - even your abilities - are always consistent with this self-image..... 2. Self-image can be changed." M. Maltz Psycho-cybernetics.

What Maltz goes on to say is that the unhappy, or failure-type personality cannot develop a new self-image purely by will power or by simply deciding to. There must be some event or some reason that provides the stimulus to decide that the old picture of the self is in error, and a new one is appropriate. You must feel that the new self-image is based on truth.

What you must do now is examine where any negative self-images are located, and decide how and by whom they were planted in your psyche. Look at some of the barriers we identified to help you identify these. From there, we can begin to replace them with a more appropriate view. We will work on this over the next couple of chapters. However, first, we will learn why we cannot just use "willpower" and "self-control" to overcome a negative self-image and any associated bad habits.

Why Willpower is Overrated and How to stop feeding your bad habits

- **Temptation**

People who are bad at resisting temptation have insufficient willpower. This is a perspective with deep cultural and moral roots, going back to Adam and Eve and the original sin. On the other hand, people who have willpower are associated with success. They stick to diets, stay slim, healthy, and wealthy. They achieve goals and success through their willpower.

Well, I have news for you: Anyone that relies solely on their willpower is going to fail. And fail big.

This is probably a massive shock, and you are wondering what evidence I have to back it up, and how we can account for such a long-standing and major misapprehension. Self-discipline and willpower is a minor industry of itself; there are going to be some quite upset people out there. However, I can substantiate my claim, and offer you some insight into how this strengthens your chances of achieving your financial goals and mastering yourself.

First, we will look at some of the evidence that reinforces the mores around willpower and self-control.

• The Willpower Experiments

Interest in willpower, the ability to avoid temptation, escalated in the 1960s after the legendary psychologist, Walter Mischel, introduced his famous "marshmallow experiment" which investigated the subject of delayed gratification.

The experimental design is very straightforward. A researcher offers a child one marshmallow to have right away, but also explains that they can have two marshmallows if they delay eating the first for about twenty minutes.

As you might expect, many young children succumb immediately or very quickly, but others hold out for the two treats. Long term studies that followed the subjects found that those that could delay gratification tended to be more successful later in life.

A second influential experiment ran in 2004. It posited that "People are happiest and healthiest when there is an optimal fit between self and environment, and this fit can be substantially improved by altering the self to fit the world" and it used a questionnaire on self-control to rate people.

"Those self-report scales are significant; they predict 'the good life' " said Michael Inzlicht, a University of Toronto psychologist who studies self-control, in early 2018. People who score highly on this scale have better relationships, are better at abstaining from binge eating and alcohol, do better in school, and are generally happier. (A 2012 meta-analysis with more than 32,648 participants found compelling evidence that these links are reliable.)

For many years, Inzlicht explains, psychologists assumed that the self-control measured by the questionnaire, evaluated the same thing (or something overlapping) as the behavioral tests of willpower. However, Inzlicht and his team wanted proof: Do these two measurements of self-control correlate to one another? People who claim they are good at self-control in the broad sense (and have positive life outcomes to prove it) are they good at summoning willpower?

There is now an increasing number of studies that debunk this connection between stated will power and behavioral evidence. Take a 2011 study published in the Journal of Personality and Social Psychology, which tracked 205 people for one week in Germany. The study participants were given BlackBerrys that would go off at random, asking them questions about self-control, their desires, and the temptations they were experiencing. What emerged was that the people who said they were good at self-control were actually not tempted in the first place. Thus they did not actually exercise restraint; they didn't experience the conflict in the first place.

- **Avoiding temptation**

Following this and other experiments, Mischel himself and many other researchers have arrived at a somewhat more modern and nuanced view. Essentially, the idea is that the key to self-control is not to be found by exercising a reservoir of willpower, but in redefining the objects of your desire.

A story from Mischel's own life may help explain his perspective. For years, the legendary psychologist was recognized as the world's foremost expert on self-control. But ironically, Mischel smoked three packs of cigarettes a day. He had tried multiple times to quit, but by his own admission, he was spectacularly unsuccessful in resisting the urge to indulge.

One day, when Mischel was visiting the medical school at Stanford University, he happened to encounter a patient suffering from an advanced form of lung cancer. In an instant, that experience changed the way the pioneering psychologist looked at cigarettes. As Mischel explained, I changed the objective value of the cigarette. It went from something I craved to something disgusting." Since then, he never smoked again.

This experience changed Mischel's take on the marshmallow experiment too. He noticed that kids that delayed gratification tended to avoid eye contact with the treat and turned their attention elsewhere. Mischel also learned that they changed the way they valued the marshmallow.

As science writer Maria Konnikova explains "Mischel has consistently found that the crucial factor in delaying gratification is the ability to change your perception of the object or action you want to resist."

How can we use the experience and evidence from the diet industry?

I would like to use this as evidence because it is so relatable. Many people have tried dieting or limiting the foods they eat either directly themselves or through a partner or parent.

When starting on a diet regime, most people start off losing weight, but not all, then some drop by the wayside, and even those that reach their goals (initially), usually regain most or all of the weight. Typically, their previous (pre-diet) trajectory of slow weight gain is resumed until the next diet.

When we look at how people behave on diets, we can see

that the emphasis is almost exclusively on how much and what they eat. To enforce this, they rely almost entirely on the "willpower" of the dieter. The average dieter is continually surrounded by temptations as they go about their normal routines, but as we have seen, willpower is a finite resource, and it is wearing and mentally draining to deploy it all the time.

Lazy and Creatures of Habit

One of the most telling studies looked at levels of obesity in the population and concluded that there was a direct link between obesity and the proximity and density of fast food outlets. Actually, this shouldn't be a shock. If every day you walk or drive past a row after row of easy, quick delicious (to our fat and sugar craving primal brains) food places, then every day you have to fight the temptation. Often you are going to succumb.

One of our primal instincts is to put in the minimum effort to save energy – which we now define as being lazy. Secondly are also disposed to be creatures of habit, because this makes for fast and generally successful decision making.

Successful dieters will adopt two strategies that seek to overcome.

- Change your habits to remove or reduce the need to exercise self-control.

For example, remove all unhealthy items from your house, if you have to go to the effort of leaving the house, the trade-offs will be much less appealing. Send someone else to get the groceries. Don't drive by the doughnut shop on the way home, go the long way.

- Perceive your desires differently.

For example, when offered a cupcake or other high sugar foodstuff, conjure an image of black, rotten, decaying teeth. (Think Tudor queen Elizabeth 1).

Changing and reframing our financial habits

The same problems and solutions apply to our financial affairs as they do to our health. We need to change our habits to be successful in meeting our financial goals. As we discussed earlier, our habits are like automated programs that once they are triggered, they become difficult to stop. Therefore, avoiding the triggers is a very successful strategy for replacing bad habits with good.

For example, don't go to the mall. If you go, then you will face temptation and probably fail. Arrange to do something else.

Late at night, maybe after a drink, you tend to go 'shopping' on Amazon. All dieters know that drinking is inimical to dieting; it can be the same with financial discipline. Therefore, don't rely on willpower, instead, rely on planning. Get a picture of the most wasteful or embarrassing thing you ever bought after a 'spree' and stick that picture on top of your laptop or computer. The 'pain' of that experience will flashback and hopefully prevent you from logging in.

There are many similar situations where planning and preparation will prevent any temptation of your financial willpower. For instance, taking a packed lunch instead of buying out. To meet your financial goals, therefore, the trick is to identify your problem habits and develop an alternative strategy that doesn't rely on willpower.

Change Your Philosophy – Change Your Life!

All the decisions we make tend to shape us and ultimately define us as people. Here, I refer more to the small micro-decisions than major macro ones, because every day we make hundreds of decisions based around our core beliefs, but we only make a dozen or so significant decisions in our entire life. So, these small decisions add up to something far more critical in defining the path we take. These core beliefs then amount to our personal philosophy of life.

So, the purpose of this section is to introduce you to a healthy financial philosophy that can replace unhealthy desires of consumerism. What we need is a philosophy for living, a set of core beliefs that will underpin our decisions and help to deliver our financial and life goals, because these are bound together.

There is a branch of philosophy created for us: Stoicism. The purpose of this philosophy is to make us happier, more resilient, more virtuous, and wiser. In turn, we will be better people, better parents, and better professionals. For some people, it conjures up a clear image of suffering in silence. However, this is nothing short of a parody for it is a living, vibrant philosophy designed to be applied and tested in the real world.

Stoicism, as a philosophy, has been practiced by emperors, kings, presidents, artists, writers, and entrepreneurs: Marcus Aurelius. Frederick the Great, George Washington, Adam Smith, John Stuart Mill, Theodore Roosevelt, General James Mattis, were all influenced by Stoic philosophy.

The Stoic school of thought was founded on the premise that an individual's emotions are solely under their control, and that one could master their emotional responses to the external events that happen around them if they wished to do so. At the core of Stoicism is the principle of separation between how the world appears to be and the individual's emotional reaction to it. This philosophy teaches that a person should learn to separate things they can control (their thoughts and internal emotions) from those that are beyond their control (external events happening in the world). It is only by doing so that one can lead a 'good' life.

Let's take the example of junk food. A stoic worldview would consider people indulging in junk food as a neutral event. However, they would recognize that the desire to eat fast food is driven by our primal brain, which craves fatty food, salt, and sugars - *a quick means to get energy.* Using their rational brain, they would see that the responses of the primal brain were created for a world where these things were in short supply rather than available 24x7. So the stoic would recognize that eating this regularly is likely to cause heart disease and weight gain, and would resist their emotional impulses, recognizing that in this case, unfettered emotions are bad.

There isn't room in this book for a complete examination of the stoic virtues and principles that we might align our lives and habits, so I will confine myself to a few of the more significant points. The benefits of Stoicism can be set out in 2 promises:

The Art of Living

The first promise of Stoicism is how to live a happy and flowing life. The Stoics believe that nature wants us to become the highest versions of ourselves, 'to be good with yourself, to live in harmony with your highest self" which is Eudaimonia. Although the closest literal translation is happiness, it more accurately refers to the overall quality of your life than a temporary mood such as happiness; it is about thriving and living an optimal life.

"First say to yourself, what would you be, then do what you must do" - Epictetus, Stoic philosopher.

Emotional Resilience

The second promise of stoic philosophy consists of both the supremely happy life (called 'eudaimonia') and the preparation to deal with whatever life throws at us (ready for anything). However, we can only deal with life's challenges when we are emotionally resilient and don't let our emotions confound us.

This is why we need to make progress toward taming and overcoming disturbing desires and emotions. Tame restricting emotions (it is not the same as unemotional)

"The glitter of gold doesn't dazzle our eyes more than the flash of the sword, and that we can easily wave aside what other people crave and fear." Seneca.

Although Stoicism is a philosophy, it has a large psychological component to it. Many of its' beliefs, such as the goal to thrive as human beings go hand in hand with research in positive psychology. It is also closely aligned with the practice of cognitive, behavioral therapy.

Stoics learn what causes the negative emotions (such as compulsive spending, living for today only, or shiny object syndrome) acknowledge them, and redirect them.

For example, when we are angry or anxious, we act calmly and make rational decisions despite the anger.

4 Virtues of Stoicism

When considering how we should behave to deliver the promises of Stoicism, there are four essential values of Stoic philosophy that we need to work towards. The two key ones that I want to discuss in more detail are temperance and wisdom, and how we can use these teachings to change our behavior to a better (financial) path.

- Courage
- Temperance
- Justice
- Wisdom

"If at some point in your life, you come across anything better than justice, truth, self-control, courage—it must be an extraordinary thing indeed." Marcus Aurelius, Roman emperor and Stoic Philosopher

Courage

The most straightforward virtue is courage, although the Stoics also extend it to include endurance of pain and discomfort.

Ideally, you should have the courage to endure the discomfort of changing your habits and possibly living a more temperate, moderated life to achieve a better life.

Temperance

Temperance or moderation is about doing nothing in excess. Doing the right thing in the right amount, in the right way. Because "We are what we repeatedly do," Aristotle also said, "therefore excellence is not an act, but a habit."

In other words: Virtue and excellence become a way of living. This in turn becomes automatic as this way of life becomes a habit. In this way, via our habits, we seek to resist temptation and to avoid exercising self-control.

"Capability is confirmed and grows in its corresponding actions, walking by walking, and running by running… therefore, if you want to do something, make a habit of it." Epictetus.

If we want to be successful, happy, or great, we have to develop the capability and establish the day-to-day habits that allow this to ensue.

This is great news because it means that impressive results or enormous changes are possible without resorting to exercising our will power, which as we have already discovered, is a limited resource. Small adjustments, sound systems, the right processes; that's what it takes.

Justice

"A commitment to justice in your own acts. Which means thought and action resulting in the common good. What you were born to do." Marcus Aurelius, Meditations, 9.31

The virtue of justice can be summed up as:

- That no one does harm to another.
- That one uses common possessions as common; private as belonging to their owners.
- We are not born for ourselves alone.
- Men were brought into being for the sake of men, that they might do good to one another.
- We ought to follow nature as a guide to contribute our part to the common good.
- Good faith, steadfastness, and truth.

"For the most part, men are induced to injure others in order to obtain what they covet." Cicero, Roman statesman and philosopher.

Wisdom

"The chief task in life is simply this; to identify and separate matters so that I can say clearly to myself which are externals not under my control, and which have to do with the choices I actually control. Where then do I look for good and evil? Not to uncontrollable externals, but within myself to the choices that are my own" — Epictetus.

Wisdom ultimately informs action. There is an instant between stimulus and response. In that instant is our power to choose our response. That space is wisdom's opportunity. Recognizing that space is the first step, where we either look to our goals and apply our learning, or we throw it out the window and act impulsively and irrationally.

The perfect stoic

How would we describe a person who successfully lived their life, moment by moment, according to the highest goals in stoic philosophy, with all the Stoic virtues?

The perfect stoic lives in total harmony with themselves, the rest of humanity and nature, simply because they follow reason *(rational thought rather than emotion)* and accept their fate graciously, in as far as it is beyond their control. Moreover, they rise above irrational desires and emotions to achieve peace of mind.

How Stoicism Can Help You Manage Your Finances Better

By approaching life from a stoic perspective, you can learn how to take charge of your emotions and stamp your authority in your financial habits. Some of the important lessons that you can draw from Stoicism *(which will help you to cultivate financial discipline in your life and get rid of the tendency to overspend)* include:

i) Recognize that all Emotions Come from Within Yourself and You Have the Power to Control Them

As human beings, we tend to automatically react to things without realizing that all our emotions essentially stem from within. We often attribute how we feel to external factors such as other people, places, and events when our emotions are solely within our power and control.

Suppose you visit a store and find that a particular product that you've been thinking about buying is on sale. While you may justify the emotional reaction as a response to the product, the truth of the matter is that your feelings of desire stem from within yourself. You, therefore, have the power to control your emotions and refrain from purchasing something only because it evokes desire in you.

Mentally practicing control through imagination offers us an opportunity to train new traits and attitudes. If we practice through this method, it is almost as effective as actually performing the habit or action.

ii) Learn to Practice Moderation in Spending

We live in a world where advertisements for all kinds of products constantly bombard us. Amid all this cacophony, it is easy to think that you don't have a choice in how you spend your money. However, this is not the case. Just as we can decide how we respond to different stimuli, we can choose what to focus our attention on and consequently how we spend our money. By adopting the stoic mindset (which does not desire material possessions for their own sake, but for how they can enrich their lives in the long run), you can overcome the temptation of compulsively spending on things that you do not need.

One way to achieve this is to lie somewhere quiet and imagine yourself passing by the shops and stores without entering or spending any money. Repeat this frequently, and the imagination will become the reality.

iii) Realize that failure is not the End of your Life

One of the things that usually keep us from reaching our goals is the fear of failure. Ruminating over worst-case scenarios can paralyze you with fear and diminish confidence in your abilities to achieve your goals. This essentially causes you to fail without even trying. A stoic will recognize and accept the fact that failure is a fact of life. Those that have not failed have not tried.

The means of responding to failure begins by not being surprised by it. The reason that so many failures set us back (failed relationships, failed businesses, failed attempts to stop spending) is that we never consider that things could happen any other way but the way we wanted them to.

The Stoics spent a lot of time practicing 'negative visualization'—thinking about what could go wrong, what the worst-case scenario was, what would be outside their control. They did this to eliminate unpleasant surprises. They also do it so they can go into every situation with their eyes wide open, so they can properly adjust for or prevent a potential failure. The wise man is aware of all possibilities and prepares for all of them. In this way, there is no such thing as failure - simply outcomes.

In summary, here are some of the key points that you should take away from this chapter, along with some actions that you should perform

- In order to achieve financial success, it is imperative that you identify the psychological barriers and your bad spending habits.
- Analyze your self-image about your attitude to money, spending, and investing, and try to find the root cause of this view, when and how did it start?
- Think about all the times you identified as lacking willpower or even having strong self-control and start to think about how you reframe these experiences
- How can you avoid the circumstance where you are tempted, for example
- Think about how the values of Stoicism apply to yourself and could they transform some of your habits and attitudes? If you believe in some new principles, it will begin to replace your self-image with new values.

CHAPTER FOUR: MAKING CHOICES AND CREATING POSITIVE CHANGES

The last chapter was about preparing our state of mind, ready to allow us to move on to the next phase. This chapter is concerned with deciding what you want to achieve from your financial makeover. It describes the process of turning these desires into a tangible plan for action that is going to be successful in making positive changes in your life - changes that you can live with and which will deliver your aspirations.

In this chapter, you will learn:

- Why it is important to have goals
- How to create clear goals that can be actioned and tracked (SMART goals)
- How to use your imagination to develop a vision of what success will be like for each goal.
- How to use psychological techniques to strengthen your chances of success
- Common reasons why you could fail to change your habits and not meet your goals

- Finally, the importance of communication where money and relationships are concerned.

In order to become more responsible in the way you spend your money, you need to change your mindset and develop new healthy habits that will help you to prioritize your spending more effectively, and get rid of the tendency to compulsively buy things you don't need. By achieving the balance of purpose and pleasure through your spending, you can greatly improve not only your discipline in the way you spend your money, but also enhance your quality of life significantly. In this chapter, we are going to look at the importance of setting financial goals and some of the ways in which you can effect positive changes in your money habits to achieve success.

Why do We Need to Set Goals?

Through setting properly defined goals, we can orient ourselves towards our dreams and take the necessary steps that push us closer towards our objectives in life. In other words, goals provide us with purpose and give us targets to strive towards. 'Purposefulness' is one of the two dimensions of happiness, the other being 'pleasure'. Goals are the expression of desires and define the purpose of our life. Our actions are given meaning and purpose by our goals.

Without setting goals, therefore, it can be difficult to have any purpose in our lives, and conversely, without purpose, the only way to achieve happiness is through pleasure. The hedonistic lifestyle, which is purely pleasure-driven, is deeply unsatisfying for most people because it is so one-sided.

As Maltz observes in Psycho-Cybernetics, the conscious mind directs the unconscious mind, which acts as an automatic goal striving machine. "It will work automatically and impersonally to achieve goals of success and happiness, or unhappiness and failure, depending on the goals that you self set for it. Present it with 'success goals', and it functions as a success mechanism. Present it with negative goals, and it operates as a failure mechanism."

If you are trying to achieve financial success, therefore, here are some of the reasons why you need to set goals.

- Goals Enable You to Take Control of Your Life

Most people tend to go through life without having a clear objective of what they hope to achieve. This often leads to disillusionment despite the hard work and effort they may be putting in their lives. Failing to set goals can cause you to spend your life aimlessly without ever achieving anything meaningful. However, through setting realistic and actionable goals, you are able to break out of automated habits and begin to organize your life the way you envision it.

- Goals Allow You to Focus

While having a life purpose provides you with a general direction of where you are going, your goals enable you to focus on specific areas where you need to channel your efforts to achieve your overall purpose. Moreover, goals help you to zero in on the important things that you should pay attention to.

We all have goals, whether they are recognized or not - even the alcoholic and the drug addict. We can either move towards our conscious desired goals or drift towards our unconscious, possibly undesired, goals.

Let us suppose for a moment that you are trying to establish a restaurant business. In the beginning, you may not have all the details on how to achieve this. You should not worry about the 'how' at this stage. Through setting goals and subgoals, you can acquire a focal point and determine how best to approach your venture. You may begin by figuring out the dishes and cuisines that are popular in your locality and learning how to make them. You can also test the different recipes and let your friends or family try them out and provide you with feedback. Slowly you move towards your target goal as you achieve each subgoal.

- Goals Promote Accountability

Setting goals enables you to be accountable to yourself. Instead of simply talking about what you hope to achieve, goals oblige you to act, which is what will ensure that you succeed. Since your goals are personal and only relevant to yourself and family, having specific targets allows you to easily track your progress and gauge whether you are working towards your set objectives.

- Goals Help to Minimize Procrastination

When you set targets for yourself, you essentially *make yourself accountable to yourself.* You realize that you have a given time frame to achieve certain milestones, and are therefore able to follow through with your goals. This is in contrast to when you do things based on a sudden feeling or whim, in which case, there is little pressure on yourself, and you are therefore more likely to think that it doesn't matter when you will achieve something, therefore you never achieve it. Goals, therefore, act as drivers that keep you on your toes to ensure that you don't procrastinate.

- Goals Help to Build Self-Confidence

From time to time, we all have dreams that may seem impossible to achieve. However, setting goals enables us to break down our vision into smaller, manageable tasks that are much easier to navigate. Each time we achieve one of the smaller goals, it boosts our confidence and helps to spur us on. This can help to inspire and motivate us to take action even when you are overwhelmed with challenges that seem insurmountable. For example, if your goal is to raise money for investing in an income-generating enterprise, you can start by cutting down on your monthly expenditure and put the freed-up funds in a savings or investment account. As your funds begin to increase, you will become more confident in your ability to raise the outstanding amount for your business enterprise.

How do We Set Goals?

For you to attain financial success, you need to know how to set realistic and actionable goals. The kind of goals that you set for yourself ought to clearly outline the reason why they exist, the steps that you need to follow, as well as the time-frame in which you will achieve them.

Set SMART Goals. The SMART goal criteria is a handy tool that can help you to set and achieve your financial goals. The acronym SMART stands for Specific, Measurable, Attainable, Relevant, and Timely.

- Specific Goals

When setting goals, you need to be clear about what you hope to achieve. Having clearly defined and unambiguous goals increase the chances of succeeding. If your goals are too generalized, you may end up having a difficult time figuring where to begin or how to accomplish key milestones. Instead of thinking, *"I want to be rich"* for instance, a specific goal would be something like *"I want to save $10,000 by the end of the year to start my own small business."*

There are several questions that you need to consider when setting specific goals. These include:

- What exactly are you trying to achieve? *(this ought to be as detailed as possible)*

- Why do you want to pursue the goal *(purpose)*

- Who needs to be involved? *(this is important if you are working with other people)*

- When do you plan to achieve it? *(time-frame)*

- Where do you hope to achieve this goal *(location)*

- Measurable Goals

A SMART goal needs to have criteria for measuring and tracking progress. Without having this, it can be challenging to determine whether you are achieving any milestones. Some of the questions to consider when setting measurable goals include:

- How do I know if I am making progress

- What are the milestones that I need to achieve to succeed in my goal

For example, if you are putting money into a savings plan to have a down payment of $100,000 for a house that you intend to mortgage, you can define your goal as saving a particular amount of money, say $2,000 every month. This means it will take you slightly over four years to raise this money. By splitting your goal into smaller, measurable units, you will be able to keep track of your progress simply by checking how much money you have saved at the end of every month.

- Achievable Goals

When setting goals, it is very important to evaluate whether they are realistically attainable. This involves evaluating the costs *(time, money, and effort)* that you are likely to incur and weighing them against the benefits you are likely to reap as well as any other obligations you may have in life. If you don't have the resources that are required to achieve a certain goal, you are less likely to succeed. This doesn't mean that you shouldn't aspire for lofty goals that seem beyond reach. After all, with the right planning, patience, and dedication, you can achieve goals that some may consider impossible. However, it is always good to assess whether you have the tools that are required to attain specific goals, and in case they are lacking, you must figure out how to acquire them.

- Relevant Goals

It is very important to ensure that the goals you set are relevant to you as a person. In other words, do they align with your values? Are they compatible with your personality? For your goals to be meaningful, you need to be able to answer these questions. Setting relevant goals will motivate and prompt you to take actionable steps towards achieving them.

- Timely Goals

While setting goals is relatively easy, unless your goals have a defined time-frame, they will likely not come to fruition. This is because you will be much more likely to procrastinate and put off doing things at the right time. As a result, your goals may end up stalling. You should, therefore, have clearly defined timelines and deadlines and strive to work within these constraints. This will not only motivate you to work harder towards your goals, but also instill a sense of accountability, which will ensure you follow through on your vision.

An example of a SMART goal would be as follows: *I want to retire (stop being employed) at 60 (in 10 years), with a pension pot of $500,000.*

How to Build a Powerful Vision

It is easy to set goals, but to translate them into actions via our conscious and then our unconscious, we need to have a strong desire. That is to say, the reason "why", the motivation, or the desire behind the goal. We call this the "vision" - it is the fuel for the goal. Having a strong vision is absolutely vital when it comes to setting goals since it justifies our goals. Without a clear, meaningful, and powerful vision, you will not generate the desire or motivation to follow through on your goals.

The process of creating this "vision", which Maltz calls our "Creative Mechanism", simply involves the use of our imagination. In this case, the more vivid your imagination, the better, as it is the vividness of your vision, it's meaning to you, that will define its power.

To Maltz, goal and vision were one and the same thing, but we have deliberately drawn a distinction between the two. The reason for this is that the goal can be written down and expressed and understood by other people.

However, the "vision" as we explain it here, is very personal to you.

Remember that we can either use our imaginations constructively or destructively. So, it is far better to put them to work constructively so that we automate our behaviors towards success. The psychological effect is closely related to how hypnosis or neuro-linguistic-programming (NLP) work. That is to say that if we believe something to be true, then we will act commensurately. For example, someone hypnotized to believe they are standing naked at the North Pole will display physical symptoms of suffering from cold, such as shivering and goose-bumps. This is the potential power of your "vision" on your behavior.

To build our vision, we need to imagine what life will be like once we have achieved our goal. This is why I called it a 'vision,' since it is a look into the future via your imagination. If your goal is to pay off your mortgage and be debt-free, then it is not enough to picture a letter arriving from your bank saying that you cleared your loan. This will have no resonance. What you must do is build a full picture of what it will feel like and what you will be able to do once you are mortgage-free. How else will your life be at that time? Will the kids be running around the yard playing? Will there be a dog and a cat? Are you growing yellow roses around the door? How do they smell? Will it mean you can retire and devote time to your hobbies? Have you built that pizza oven you always planned - are pizzas cooking? What is happening on the street? Use all your senses; sight, hearing, smell, and touch to build your vision.

Do not forget about feelings; these are powerful too. How will you feel when you are mortgage-free? Will you jump for joy and hug? Will you throw a big party for family and friends?

The more details you can populate into your vision, the

more real it will seem, and the more powerfully it will act to drive your desire and actions. Thinking about your goals in terms of how their benefits will raise your motivation to succeed with your goals in spite of the challenges you may experience.

> *"When your will and your imagination are in conflict then imagination invariably wins the day"* Emile Coue, French pharmacist/psychologist.

It is not enough to simply have your vision in your mind - the second step is to make it more tangible and real. You can do so by creating a vision board, where you put images, photos, newspaper cutouts, and other visual representations of your dream. By having this visual element to your vision and looking at it daily, you will become constantly aware of your goals. If helpful, create a drawing of your vision. If you cannot find any other visualization, then write down your goals. You can put these on display somewhere that you will see them frequently (such as the fridge) to remind you of them and the reasons you created them.

Techniques to Reinforce Your Goals and Vision

Although setting goals is quite easy to do, it can be challenging to achieve your goals if you are not motivated enough. We live in a world that has more distractions than ever before, thanks to technology. It can be very tempting to simply give in to the easier option, particularly when we run into challenging situations. However, by taking the easy route or giving up on your goals, you will end up not making any progress in things that you want to achieve in life. To remain focussed and consistent with your goals, therefore, you need to have a constant fuel of motivation. Here are some of the ways in which you can motivate yourself to follow through with your goals.

Commit Your Goals in Writing

While there is nothing wrong with conceptualizing your goals and organizing them mentally, writing them down makes them seem more tangible and real. Without having a written record of your goals, you can easily get sidetracked by your everyday routines and events, which may cause you to forget about them altogether. When writing down your goals, it is always best to use positive language that has an outcome. For instance, if you are trying to cut down on your overspending, say *"I'm going to save $500 this month to invest"*. Framing your goals in a positive way relieves you of unnecessary pressure and makes the goal seem appealing. This can provide you with the motivation to overcome the psychological challenges that are holding you back from achieving success. If your subconscious is still saying *"I'm going to sacrifice a lot this month and miss out on fun activities."*, then you must replace this with a positive vision of the end state where you achieve financial freedom, or whatever is the desired outcome. You will also have to be more creative in creating other goals that fill your time productively, but that don't involve spending money. There are a surprising number of these things, once you look and think!

How to Use Public Commitment to Strengthen Your Commitment to Your Goals

Public commitment typically entails making public the personal goals that you have set for yourself. Unlike private commitments, which rely on self-accountability and discipline, public commitments are usually more effective at managing behavior. This is because everyone has a powerful subconscious desire to appear consistent with statements and promises they have made. This desire arises from socialisation and normative behaviour that has been reinforced in us since infancy. Think about this image and the things that are said about people who don't live up to their commitments. They are called liars, welchers, spineless and worse. This is consistent across time and cultures, hence its power.

Public commitments can, therefore, provide a powerful incentive for individuals to regulate their behavior and remain focussed on their goals.

If you are trying to achieve a financial goal, say reduce your spending and save money, you can greatly benefit from making a public commitment to this goal. For instance, you can inform your friends and family about all the money you are going to save from cutting down on unnecessary spending on things like entertainment, drinks, and expensive restaurant meals. Then the knowledge they may ask about your progress will help you to keep track of your spending and saving, or having to lie your friends and family. In this way, you will be able to inculcate self-discipline, which will help you to stick with your goals even when temptations to do otherwise arise.

Review your Goals and Visions

One of the most critical things that you must do to reinforce your chances of success is to review your goals regularly. How regularly depends on the size of the goal. For example, it doesn't make sense to review a goal (to retire in 10 years with a $500,000 pension pot) every day. It does make sense to review that at least every year. This enables you to check whether you are on or off- track, and adjust any needed actions. Conversely, if you have a goal to save $2,000 in three months, then you need to check this every week or every day. However, this is where it is essential that the big goals are supported by smaller goals that are all leading in the right direction since you can meaningfully check the smaller goals frequently.

The other benefit of regularly checking your goals is to reaffirm your desire to achieve them. Every time you think about your goal and recall your vision, it will help to motivate your subconscious towards achieving it. Remember, it is your subconscious that is going to help you avoid those tricky self-control/willpower problems by enabling you to reframe your desire or to distract from the issue.

This again, is where a strong vision sitting in your imagination is important. Each time you review your goal, you should also refresh your vision so that you remember what it is that you desire, and the reasons why you are striving for that goal. Each time you use your imagination to *feel* that desire, you reinforce your goal at a subconscious level. The more you practice this, just like anything else, the stronger your desire will become.

"Arouse deep desire for these things. Become enthusiastic about them. Dwell on them and keep going over them in your mind."
Maltz, Psycho-Cybernetic

Positive reinforcement

Positive reinforcement is a strategy that involves promising yourself a reward for desirable behavior. Employing positive reinforcement in your goals provides you with the incentive to follow through with them, thus helping you to realize your vision.

Moreover, it is worth noting that success tends to have a snowball effect, which essentially means that once you take the initial steps towards your goals, everything begins to fit into place, and your success grows exponentially.

If one of your goals is to pay off debt, then make sure you keep charts of your progress (perhaps like those for public appeals for funds) and display them somewhere prominently.

Set Big Goals

As counterintuitive as it may seem, setting huge goals with big rewards can provide more motivation than small ones. This does not necessarily mean that your goals have to be expensive. On the contrary, they should simply be goals that excite you and inspire you to work hard. The higher the stake, the more motivated you will feel about pursuing your goals. It is also easier to create an impactful and effective vision around big goals, that is simply not possible with small goals.

Break Down Your Big Goals into Smaller goals

Having said that, the big goals will need to be supported by smaller goals. Bigger goals, especially long-term ones, may seem quite intimidating if you think about the time, money, and effort that you will need to put in. This can cause you to feel discouraged and unmotivated. However, by breaking your goals into smaller actionable tasks and setting achievable deadlines, you will be able to track progress on your big goals. So create a big goals with an effective vision of what you will achieve, and then create lots of supporting goals that are going to get you there , but that you can achieve more quickly and meaningfully track the progress.

Why do we Fail to Achieve our Goals?

Setting goals provides us with a direction in life and gives us a clear vision of what we need to do to succeed. Whenever we achieve our goals, our self-confidence increases, and we feel inspired to set bigger ones. However, there are several factors that may hinder us from achieving our goals. These include:

- Ensure Your Incentive is Meaningful

When it comes to positive reinforcement, you have complete control over the incentive you choose for your goals. You need to select a reward that is meaningful to you since this will boost your motivation to achieve your goals. If your aim is to cut down on your spending and save money, for example, you can treat yourself (some ice cream, for example) every time you manage to meet your targets.

- Set Specific Goals

Most people tend to set goals that are vague and non-specific. For instance, they may decide that they want to get rich or adopt a healthy lifestyle. However, without having a clearly defined goal, it can be difficult to determine the right strategy to apply to achieve that goal.

So, instead of simply saying you want to be rich, it might be more useful to have a specific target in mind, for example, raising $10,000 to start a business. By outlining your goal clearly, and following the SMART method it will be easier to come up with a plan of action that will help you to achieve your set objectives.

- Lack of Focus

To achieve your goals and realize your dreams, you need

to focus on making the right decisions and actions. While it is okay to have plenty of goals, you should identify those that are most important to you and focus on achieving them first. After all, there is no point in having numerous goals if you are unable to achieve even one.

- Giving too Many Excuses

Very often, we fail to achieve our goals because we keep on coming up with excuses about why we can't do what we are supposed to do. Excuses are usually the blame we attach to external factors instead of ourselves. However, very often, these factors are within our ability to influence or adopt an alternative strategy. This is why the stoic will not assume that things will go to plan, and will be ready to adapt. Instead of pushing us towards our goals, excuses only serve the purpose of evading personal responsibility and distracting us from our vision. Although it is easier to do nothing rather than tackling what you need to do, you must overcome the tendency to make excuses for yourself since this will keep you stuck and prevent you from reaching your goals. Our stoic philosophy tells us there is no failure, only outcomes.

- Don't Worry Over What You Can't Control

Very often, we tend to worry too much about how the future is going to unfold, and whether we will be able to achieve the goals that we have set out to accomplish. But always overthinking about things that are beyond your control can kill your motivation. You may even find yourself questioning whether your goals are worth pursuing. However, this mindset is not helpful, and will only serve to derail you from your goals. Instead of worrying too much about what you can't control, switch your focus on things that can push you closer towards your goals.

As Maltz says *"Do not be afraid of making mistakes, or of temporary failures. All servo mechanisms achieve a goal by negative feedback, or by going forward, making mistakes, and immediately correcting course."*

Relationships and Money

Money issues are, without a doubt, some of the most common challenges that relationships face today. Money is one of the leading causes of fights in relationships, second only to infidelity. To build a robust and healthy relationship with your partner or spouse, therefore, it is necessary to learn how to manage your financial life as a team. Here are some of the ways in which you can improve how you manage your finances in partnership with your spouse.

i) Learn about Your Partner's Money Habits

Ideally, you should familiarize yourself with your partner's spending habits early in your relationship. One way in which you can do this is by having regular financial quizzes where both of you list how much you have spent or saved over a given duration and tallying the answers. Based on your findings, you can then have discussions to address any financial issues that you have identified and brainstorm possible solutions.

ii) Check Whether Your Goals are Compatible

One of the best ways to gauge your partner's financial mindset in a non-threatening or invasive way is to discuss long-term goals. Does your partner plan to retire soon? Are they thinking about switching careers? How do they feel about going on vacation? Do they want children in the future? If so, how many? Openly sharing your long-term goals will help you to align your financial vision and develop a workable strategy that will help both of you to realize your dreams.

iii) Find an Arbiter

If you find yourself continually clashing with your partner over finances, you may want to enlist a referee such as a financial advisor or financial counselor. This neutral party will be able to weigh in on your dispute and help you to come up with meaningful solutions to get you on the same page. Arranging for regular meetings with your financial referee will help you to raise any concerns that you may have, and allow you to reach a consensus with your partner on the best way forward.

iv) Work with Your Partner to Set and Share Goals

In case you are in a long-term relationship or married, it is important to collaborate with your partner when it comes to setting financial goals. If your financial objectives are conflicting, this may lead to incompatible financial habits, which may breed discontent and resentment in your relationship. For instance, if your partner is a compulsive spender who always uses money extravagantly, it might be challenging for you to save money and invest in a property. This disconnect between your financial goals is likely to drive a wedge in your relationship and lead to conflict. For this reason, it is vital to work together with your partner and set goals that are mutually beneficial. This will open up the channel for communication, and you will be able to reach a consensus on the right goals to pursue.

Moreover, by involving your partner in your financial vision, you will not only feel more connected but also forge an actionable plan on how to succeed in your vision.

In summary, here are some of the main takeaways from this chapter:

- Learning how to set SMART goals is crucial when it comes to organizing your financial life since it provides you with a framework to base your vision around.
- Visualizing your success will provide you with inspiration and motivation to pursue your goals even when you encounter challenges along the way
- Making a public commitment to your goals helps build accountability and prevents the tendency of procrastinating.
- You should make it your priority to create shared goals with your spouse/partner to align your financial vision, plan accordingly, and execute your actions in a coordinated way.
- You are now ready to start drawing up your own SMART goals and accompany these with your visions of success, which you can bring to life with, for example, pictures and a pinboard.

CHAPTER FIVE: THE OUTCOME YOU NEED TO ACHIEVE NOW, WHICH WILL LEAD TO FINANCIAL PROSPERITY

"Discipline is just choosing between what you want now and what you want most" Abraham Lincoln

IF YOU ARE TIRED OF BEING BROKE AND ARE TRYING TO restore financial sanity in your life, you must begin making the right changes in your spending immediately. Unless you take back control of your money, you will continue to reinforce the bad habits that have been holding you back from achieving financial prosperity. One of the essential practices that you need to incorporate in your spending habits is budgeting. In this chapter, we are going to look at what budgeting entails, why it is important, and how you can use a budget to create surplus income.

What is a Budget and Why do You Need One?

As human beings, we tend to have unlimited wants that can't be fully satisfied by the limited resources *(income)* that are available to us. Due to this, we are forced to prioritize our wants and decide which ones should be satisfied first. Luckily, you can easily achieve this through budgeting.

A budget is essentially a plan that outlines how you intend to spend your money. Through creating a budget, you can determine in advance whether you have enough money to do the things that you intend to do. In other words, a budget enables you to balance your expenses with your income. This is very important because failure to balance these two elements can lead to overspending, which can gradually result in an accumulation of debt. In order to track your spending effectively, therefore, a budget is necessary.

Somewhere in my attic, I have a box of books, the complete records that my mother kept of the family finances for fifty years. For all her married life, she recorded every transaction of significance, and diligently reconciled bank and credit card statements. She was always on top of every penny that we spent, and she always knew our financial standing. These are probably a gold mine for anyone interested in how a working-class family spent their income fifty years ago.

7 Benefits of Having a Budget

Budgeting is one of the best ways of managing your money. However, many people often avoid creating budgets because they feel like it is an additional chore to the numerous tasks they have to carry out regularly. While budgeting might seem like an extra burden, there are plenty of reasons why having a budget will benefit you.

- It Gives You Total Control over Your Finances

Let's face it, if you are not in control of your money, then it means that it is controlling you. Budgeting allows you to become more intentional in your spending and saving, thus providing you with greater control over your money. By creating a budget, you can eliminate the stress of suddenly requiring to adjust your funds due to unplanned expenses. In addition to this, budgeting enables you to decide which short term sacrifices to make to reap long term benefits. For instance, you can opt to forgo the cup of coffee that you grab every day at the coffee shop and put that money in a savings fund for a vacation trip.

- It Enables You to Stay Focussed on Your Financial Goals

Another key advantage of a budget is that it helps you to minimize impulsive buying of products that can put a serious dent in your finances. So, if you earn a fixed income, preparing a spending budget will help you to meet your day-to-day expenses much easier.

- It Allows You to Track Your Income and Spending

Budgeting provides you with a complete understanding of your finances, and this enables you to have more control over your money. By making a budget, you are able to know where your money is coming from every month, where you are spending it, and how much is left. This allows you to make informed decisions and plan your spending more effectively.

- It Allows You to Cushion Against Unexpected Emergencies

Every now and then, we all get hit by unexpected

expenses, which can take up a considerable chunk of our finances. These may include medical emergencies, home repairs, and other unplanned events that require us to dig deep into our pockets. It is therefore important to set aside some money in an emergency fund to cater to these unprecedented events when they arise. You should ensure that you always allocate some money for savings whenever you are budgeting since doing so will help you to prepare financially for unplanned expenses.

- It Provides You with a 'Safety Net'

Job security is undoubtedly a hot topic in the world today, and with the current coronavirus pandemic that is ravaging economies and businesses around the world, many employees have already lost their jobs. With more people set to lose their livelihoods, the importance of budgeting as a safety net against economic turmoil is pushing to the fore. Having a budget enables you to adapt more quickly and with greater certainty.

- It Helps You to Minimize Unnecessary Debt

Creating and sticking to a budget helps you to ensure that you don't spend money that you don't have. Credit cards have made a lot of consumers susceptible to impulsive spending due to the convenience and feeling of freedom that they provide. As a result, many people often end up spending money they don't have on things they don't need and are left drowning in debt. Having a budget helps you to avoid getting into this situation since you can tell how much you earn, how much you are spending, and how much you are able to save.

- It Enables You to Identify Bad Spending Habits

Creating a budget forces you to look at your spending more closely, which can shed light on bad spending habits. For instance, you may notice that you spend a lot more than you should on daily take-out lunches. Your budget will help you recognize how you can cut down on these unnecessary expenses and find ways of redirecting that money to more beneficial areas such as savings or investments.

It is worth noting that for a budget to be effective, it requires conscious thought and effort on your part. Having a budget is not a magic bullet that will take away all your bad spending habits overnight. On the contrary, the purpose of a budget is to highlight your financial goals and provide you with a reference that will help you to stay committed to them. Creating a budget helps you to be aware of your spending, which in turn puts you in control over your finances. By building and sticking to a budget, you will become more intentional about your spending and cut down on unnecessary expenses. This will not only help you to minimize debt but also boost confidence in your ability to achieve financial success.

Despite the numerous benefits that budgeting provides, many people still hold the wrong notion of it being an unnecessary choice? After all, why can't you simply track your spending as you go? Well, there are several reasons why this strategy is not very useful in the long run.

First, without having a budget, it is a lot easier to fall victim to compulsive spending habits. Whenever you visit a store without having a clear plan of what you intend to purchase, there is a strong chance that you will be lured by advertised or on-sale products and end up spending money on things that you hadn't planned. This can cause deficits in your income and lead to imbalances, which can be stressful to deal with. Let's suppose you visit a store and find that a new stylish TV set is on sale. While you hadn't planned to purchase this device on this occasion, you may be lured by the display and end up spending money that you had put in your savings account to acquire this TV. This will put a dent in your surplus income and leave you vulnerable in case of an emergency. Even though you have a budget, you should still apply the rules of spending before making a purchase.

- Can I afford it?
- Do I need it?
- Is it peaceful /virtuous - in harmony with your life?

Moreover, without building a budget, you lack a clear picture of your income and spending habits, which can wrongly cause you to assume that you have too much cash flow. For instance, looking at your checking account balance without a budget gives you a misleading picture of your financial health if you've forgotten that large bill coming up. This can make it difficult to prioritize your spending according to your income and may lead to misallocation of funds.

Why You Need to Create a Surplus in Your Budget

A budget surplus occurs when you have more income than expenses during a given period (of one week, one month, or a year). Budget surpluses arise when you have income left over after all expenses during a certain period. In contrast, when there is a deficit, *(expenses exceed available income),* then the result is ***debt***.

Here are some of the advantages of having a budget

surplus, and why you should always strive to create one in your budget.

i) It Provides You with Greater Flexibility

Having a budget surplus allows you to meet any emerging expenses. You will be able to draw from your pool of 'free' money and meet any financial obligations that may arise due to unplanned events. This provides you with greater control over your finances and makes it possible to organize your spending more efficiently. For example, let's suppose you only use 90 percent of your total budgeted income every month. This means that you have 10 percent left over, which you can decide to put in a savings plan. If you stick to this every month, you will end up accumulating a lot of surplus income, which you can use to meet other financial goals.

ii) It Helps to Inculcate Financial Discipline

A regular budget surplus is essentially an indication that one has excellent financial discipline. In other words, it shows that you are planning and spending your income well. Having good financial discipline is important because it minimizes your risk of accumulating debt and increases your chances of securing credit at favorable interest rates. Lenders often evaluate one's ability to manage finances properly when considering whether or not to advance credit to them. So, by creating a surplus in your budget, you improve your credit-worthiness significantly.

iii) It Promotes Investment

Creating a surplus in your budget allows you to take advantage of investment opportunities whenever they arise. If you are planning to start a small business, for instance, you can use your accumulated budget surplus as seed capital for your venture, thus minimizing the need for credit from external investors. This can help you to avoid debt and improve your financial standing.

While building a budget surplus might seem like a frugal and constraining process, the numerous benefits that it accords you make it worth doing. There are plenty of people who have been able to improve their financial status simply by creating surplus income through budgeting. Take the example of Mike. For a very long time, Mike had been struggling to stay afloat with the $1800 per month salary that he receives from his cashier job. While this income can sustain most of Mike's monthly expenses, including his rent, food, gas, and utilities, he always ended up running out of money before the end of the month, which forced him to rack up debt from credit card purchases. In the course of evaluating Mike's spending in one month, we discovered that he was spending at least $35 every week on take-out lunches which he would grab at a local diner.

After analyzing his situation, Mike decided to prepare packed lunches in the morning *(which he would bring to work)*, thereby cutting down on his daily expenses. He opted to put the money that he would have otherwise spent in a savings account. Within 2 months, he had saved enough money to buy a bike *(which he now uses to commute to work)* thus cutting down on transport expenditure. As a result of modifying his budget to create a surplus, Mike has been able to build a cumulative saving of $6000 within 15 months.

As you can see from this account, having a budget surplus can empower you and avail 'better' financial opportunities. Obviously, it is not easy to create a surplus, especially if you earn a modest income and are bogged down by lots of expenses. However, regardless of how much you earn, you can always find ways of building a surplus by cutting down on expenses that are not necessary and always trying to stick to the budget that you've created. By doing so, you will be able to grow your spare income which you can channel into investment opportunities that will help you to increase your earnings.

The following table illustrates the power of creating even a small budget surplus regularly and consistently. The column on the left shows what happens if you have a $100 monthly deficit (every month) which you finance on a credit card (at 29% APR). The column on the right shows what happens if you have a $100 surplus, which you invest in the stock market and grows at 12% *(which was the average growth in the S&P 500)*. As you can see after 5 years with the deficit, you end up with over $12,000 in debt, whereas the investor will have $8,000 as savings.

	Debtor	**Investor**
COST OR RETURN	20%	12%
CASHFLOW	$-100	$100
YEAR 1	$-1,374	$1,272
YEAR 2	$-3,146	$2,697
YEAR 3	$-5,433	$4,292
YEAR 4	$-8,382	$6,079
YEAR 5	$-12,187	$8,0,81

Understand Your Needs vs Wants

Once you have acknowledged the problem and made a conscious decision to change the habits that keep you broke, you need to start to differentiate between your needs and your wants. You must learn how to balance them because it provides you with clarity on where your priorities should lie. Everywhere you turn, there is an advertisement trying to convince you that you need this, that or the other product to be happy. In the midst of all this pressure, it is very easy to blur the line between what is necessary for your survival and what you desire simply because it seems appealing.

So, what exactly is the difference between a 'need' and 'want'?

Well, needs or necessities are essentially those things that you cannot live without. Think about nourishment, shelter, and good health. All these things are not only absolutely essential for your survival. Lacking any of these can make life extremely uncomfortable, and in most cases, impossible. If you have ever gone a few days without food or had to sleep out in the cold because you were homeless, you can certainly understand why these things are necessary for life. Arguably one of the main characteristics of needs is that they are universal, which means they apply to every human being. These necessities are so important that they are even recognized as basic human rights, which should be granted on an ongoing basis to everyone regardless of who they are and where they come from.

However, very often, we tend to think that we 'need' certain things to be happy. Usually, most of these things are not necessary for our survival. For instance, while a good shelter is necessary to protect yourself from the vagaries of nature such as rain and sun, you do not require a 7-bedroom mansion in an expensive neighborhood to survive. This, therefore, cannot be considered as a need. In a similar vein, you need healthy and nutritious meals daily to keep your body well-nourished and protect you from illnesses. This, however, does not mean you should eat expensive five-course meals in a 4-star restaurant every day. So in these two examples, you can see the clear distinction between needs and wants. The big mansion in a high-end neighborhood and the 5-course meal are things that you may desire, but at the end of the day, you can very well survive without them and not be negatively affected in any serious way.

In general, needs typically occupy a higher position in the priorities of humans than wants. They are the most basic things we require, without which we would be gravely affected and probably be unable to continue living. If you go for too long without food, for instance, you will gradually begin to starve and possibly die in a matter of days. Likewise, if you are homeless for long, you risk getting exposed to harsh conditions like cold, which may cause you to fall seriously ill and potentially die. As you can see, needs are irreplaceable when it comes to human life.

Nevertheless, just because wants aren't essential for survival doesn't mean they are not important. As human beings, it is natural for us to desire to create a more comfortable experience of life for ourselves. The entire exercise of human existence can be summarised as a striving to survive and thrive, which is something our wants (most of them anyway) help us to do. While owning a smartphone is not necessary for your survival (you won't die without one), it allows you to communicate with people conveniently across long distances, gives you access to information through the internet, and helps you to organize your life better. You will no doubt agree then that having such a device is important, especially today when everything has pretty much become digitized.

Unlike needs, which are more or less equally important

in our lives, 'wants' tend to vary in urgency and importance depending on the unique personality and circumstances of each person. It is not uncommon for individuals' wants to change on a moment-by-moment basis. This can happen for any number of reasons. For instance, if you wake up with a strong desire to see the latest Marvel movie and do so, you will have satisfied that want. The next thing you may want to do is watch the new Netflix drama that everyone is talking about, and once you do that, you may want something else.

Another characteristic of human wants is that they are infinite. When they want something and get it, their attention shifts to something else that they want, and this process continues indefinitely. This happens because we are always trying to find new ways of making life more comfortable, exciting, and fulfilling. So, the process of trying to satisfy our every want continues forever. The only challenge that arises is that at any given moment in time, we have limited resources. This means that we have to come up with ways of satisfying as many wants as possible using the limited resources that we have at our disposal. Since some wants are competitive, we often need to make hard choices to satisfy the one which provides us with the most optimal outcome given the few resources that we have.

In order to strike a balance between your needs and wants, it is important to evaluate each according to their order of priority. You should fulfill basic necessities before you consider any other wants. It makes absolutely no sense buying a sporty car when you are starving, right? Needs naturally come first in our order of priorities, so it only makes sense for them to be catered for before one can focus on their other wants. Therefore, when planning on how to spend your income, you should first ensure that you have good nutrition, proper shelter, and adequate clothing before anything else. Once you have all of these covered, take the time to evaluate every other want to determine whether to spend money on it. Here are some of the questions that will help you gauge whether or not to spend money on something you desire

- Do I need it?
- Can I afford it?
- Does it provide some intrinsic or practical value?
- Am I better off spending my money on something else? If so, what?

Analyzing your wants from this perspective will help you to distinguish between those that are truly valuable to you from those that are simply the product of enticing advertising. Remember, when it comes to financial discipline, you want to minimize buying things that you don't need as much as possible. Otherwise, you may end up wasting too much money and getting very little value in return.

Similarly, you need to cultivate an awareness of the addictive nature of human wants. We have already seen how wants are infinite and ever-changing depending on numerous factors, including your own personality and the unique circumstances in your life at any given moment in time. So, by being conscious about your wants, you can prevent yourself from being too attached to them since doing so can lead to distress and anxiety. Cultivating a balanced view of your wants will also help you to avoid compulsive spending whenever the desire arises, and consequently allow you to minimize your debt.

It is wise to keep in mind that the dopamine hit that we experience when we buy something we want is transient and wears off quickly, as does the impact on our happiness of purchasing something. But we are left with the impact on our finances, which we may end up having to deal with long after the initial excitement has waned. At the end of the day, it is also good to remind ourselves that it is our actions that define us, not our words. Becoming conscious of this fact will enable you to make positive changes in your behavior when it comes to how you organize and spend your money.

Here is a summary of some of the key takeaways from this chapter:

- Budgeting is a fundamental practice when it comes to financial planning, and can help you to take back control of your money
- Creating and sticking to a budget will not only allows you to track your spending more easily and build surplus income but also enables you to develop better money habits
- Start to think about how you allocate your finances between needs and wants, and how you are going to create a surplus to invest.

CHAPTER SIX: HOW TO CREATE A FINANCIAL PLAN IN JUST A FEW HOURS

In the previous section, we looked at the importance of having a budget. Let us now turn our attention to the budget-making process and how you can create effective budgets regardless of your income.

Some of the basic tools that you require to create a budget include:

- Pen and paper
- Calculator
- If you have access to a computer, use a spreadsheet or use my personal financial calculator

Here is a step-by-step guide on how to create a personal budget:

- Gather all the Financial Documents that are Available to You

One of the key aspects of the budgeting process involves calculating monthly averages of expenditure and income. So, the first thing you need to do is collect all the financial statements that are relevant to this process. This includes recent utility bills, investment accounts, credit card statements, and bank statements. If you usually shop for groceries using cash, you will also need the receipts when preparing a budget. The more information you can collect, the better.

- Record all of Your Sources of Income

Whether you are in formal or informal employment, you need to record your net pay *(after taxes)* as your monthly income. You can find this information on your payslip. In case you are self-employed or have other income streams, you should also make a cumulative record of the amount you receive from them.

If your employer makes direct contributions to a pension for you, you may want to note these so you can track your investments.

- List all of Your Expenses

Once you have determined your total monthly income, write down all the expenses that you incur over the duration of a month. This includes utility payments such as water and electricity bills, food and groceries, student loans, mortgage payments, and any other costs that you incur. You should put your regular recurring and non-regular expenses in different categories so that you can plan your income accordingly to cover each depending on their order of priority. And as you already know, regular recurring expenses such as rent and groceries need to be sorted out every month *(on an ongoing basis)*, whereas non-recurring expenses like home renovations and repairs are one-time costs, which are unlikely to appear again once resolved.

- Separate Your Expenses into Categories of Fixed and Variable

Fixed expenses refer to those that stay the same every month. These include student loans, mortgage or rent payments, car loan payments, health insurance, and credit card payments. While you should include these expenses when budgeting, they are less likely to change your budget from month to month. Variable expenses, on the other hand, are those that change from month to month. These include gasoline, groceries, entertainment, and so on.

- Calculate Your Total Income and Expenses

If your total income is greater than your total expenditure, you are probably on the right path already. This essentially means that you have a budget surplus, which you can use to prop up other areas of your budget, such as a 'rainy day' fund or an investment goal. You should also use the excess income in your budget to repay any outstanding credit card debts. If you notice that your expenses exceed your total income, it means that you need to implement new changes in your spending.

- Adjust Your Expenses

Ideally, your income should be able to cater to your needs and satisfy some of your wants. If your expenses are greater than your total income, a good way of freeing up some money would be to shave off some of your variable expenses. For instance, you may choose to cut down on the number of times that you eat out. Since this expense is not essential, it will be easy to strike it out of your budget to create extra income.

- Be Realistic with Your Budget

Once you've created a budget that works for you, it is important that you try to stick with it. There is no point in allocating $50 per month for electricity if you average $100 per month over the year. It is unlikely that you will suddenly be able to halve your electric consumption, which will eventually leave you short to meet the bill and you will have to divert other items. Suddenly your whole budget will unravel. Hence the importance we attached to gathering all the information on historic expenditure.

You can find some sample budgets in chapter 7.

Common Budgeting Problems and How to Overcome Them

The secret to achieving financial success lies in effective budgeting. However, creating a budget is only the simple part - you need to be able to be consistent in how you budget and stick to it as much as possible.

Given the day-to-day challenges that we face, there are times when we may struggle to maintain a budget. Let us now look at some of the budgeting problems that can impede you from achieving your financial goals.

- Unexpected Cash Shortages

One of the common budgeting challenges that people complain about is sudden shortages in income due to delayed payment. In essence, when your salary fails to arrive on time, it can distort your budgeting mechanism. As a result, you may end up taking unplanned debt to subsidize your expenses until your paycheck arrives.

In order to overcome this problem, you need to structure your budget in a manner that accounts for delayed income. For example, you can include a 'rainy day' fund in your recurrent budget to ensure that you have something to dig into in case your payment is delayed.

- Lack of Steady Income

Many people who operate their home businesses or work freelance jobs often face the challenge of unsteady income. This certainly poses serious budgeting problems, which are surmountable nonetheless. To address this challenge, you need to set your income expectations on the low side, depending on how they fluctuate. If your income is very unstable, then you are a great candidate for zero-based budgeting *(see chapter 8)*. By building your budget from the bottom up each month, you can create a budget surplus that will provide you with a safety net and enable you to meet your expenses for the month until your next paycheck arrives.

- Rising Cost of Living

The rising cost of goods and services due to general inflation can make it difficult to budget, especially if your income is stagnant. Many items that you renew annually, for instance, phone, cable, and insurance contracts, often rise by much more than inflation. It is therefore important to factor these costs and shopping around when they come up for renewal.

- Seasonal/Periodic Expenses

There are certain seasons of the year when spending tends to increase significantly. The holiday season, for instance, is a time when people tend to spend a lot more than they do during other periods. Without planning your budget properly, you may end up overspending and 'eating' into your income for subsequent months. It is therefore advisable to start saving in advance for birthdays, Christmas holidays, and other events that may cause irregular expenditure. If you allocate some money every month for these periodic expenses, you will reduce the strain of meeting these obligations whenever they come up.

When budgeting for this type of expense, or any other annual bill (e.g car insurance), then it is good practice to make sure that this money is properly set aside in a savings account until you need it. Possibly, you might have a good app with your checking account which will enable you to create logical savings within the same physical account; this can work too.

Since we have looked at benefits and the theory of how to budget, let's turn our attention to some practical examples, and see how they tie back to the financial goals of the budget makers.

Two Example budgets

1. The Wade family

The Wade family, Jack and Jemima, is your typical, American, single-income household, with 2 kids and a spaniel. The Wades have a 5-year-old daughter and a 3-year-old son, and both just turned 30 themselves. They also run 2 older vehicles.

The Wades have some big financial goals in life, but their income is just below the average American household income. They feel trapped by their income, and don't know if they can ever really hit their goals. They have health insurance through Jack's employment with a 5% salary contribution to a 401K with a 5% matched contribution. Jemima does not work at the moment but would like to once the kids are older.

Goals

- Buy a house – need a 10% deposit of 20%
- Retire by 55 with $20k income
- Pay for kid's college

Assets

- 401k – $25,000
- Emergency Fund – $2,000
- College Savings – $2,000

Debts

The Wades are debt-free, due to their frugal living choices. The Wades' goals seem typical, but with a $40,000 salary, let's see how they are set.

PERPETUALLY BROKE: LIVING BEYOND YOUR INCOME?

INCOME

ITEM	AMOUNT
Salary 1 (net)	$2,250.00
401k (5%+match)	
Health (Covered)	

EXPENSES

HOUSEHOLD

ITEM	AMOUNT
Rent	$850.00
Local taxes	$25.00
Electric	$50.00
Water	$40.00
Gas Utility	
Phone	
Cable / internet	$40.00
Misc taxes	
Groceries	$550.00
Pharmacies	$50.00
Gas / petrol	$80.00
Pets	$10.00
Car / van finance	
Other HP loans	
Car / van servicing	$40.00
Car insurance	$40.00
Life insurance	

CHILDREN

NAME	AMOUNT
Clothes	$30.00
Shoes	$15.00
Childcare	
School	
Lunches	
pocket money	
Christmas	$30.00
Birthdays	$20.00
Sports / clubs	
Buses / transport	
Other childcare	

PERSONAL

ITEM	AMOUNT
Clothes	$30.00
Shoes	$15.00
Grooming	$15.00
Mobile x 2	$60.00
gifts	$10.00
Entertainment	
Sundry cash	$100.00
Loans / hp	
Dry cleaning	
Lunches	
Dining out	$100.00
Takeouts	
Other transport	

SUMMARY

INCOME	$2,250.00
EXPENSES	$2,200.00
NET CASH IN / OUT	$50.00
SAVINGS	$50.00
FLOAT CARRIED FORWARD	$0.00
OPENING SAVINGS BALANCE	$2,000.00
CLOSING SAVINGS BALANCE	$2,050.00

We can see that they have managed to create a small budget surplus, which is very positive. This should continue to be saved away to boost their emergency fund.

They could achieve additional savings if they were to own and run only 1 vehicle. This would give a further saving of about $500 per year (probably more) as it would be less likely to need their emergency fund for repairs.

Additional areas to look to squeeze expenditure a little would be groceries, clothes, cash, and dining out. They could also boost their income if Jemima could get a side hustle or part-time job.

Achieving their goals

- **Goal 1 – Buy a house ($200k) with a deposit of $20k**

If they get a mortgage at 4%, then they can make payments over 30 years on a $180k mortgage at about the same amount as their rent, which is just affordable. However, as things stand, they have no realistic prospect of saving a $20k deposit, and without that deposit, the loan is not likely to be affordable. This will probably have to go on the back burner until Jemima can return to working.

- **Goal 2 – Retire at 55 with an income of $20k**

To achieve an income of $20k per annum (half their current salary), which really needs to last 30 years, then they will only be able to draw about 5% pa from the fund. That implies they will need a fund of $400k. A strong history of contributions also means they are off to a very good start.

Given their current contributions and real investment

returns of 7%, they will have a pot that will only be a bit short of the target. A target of $57k or $58k is more realistic, especially if they take on a mortgage. Also, an income of $20k (maybe low) if they are having to find rent rather than owning a property outright.

- **Goal 3 – Saving for Kid's college**

Saving for the kid's college fund is currently out of reach too. However, (suggestion) they may approach their grandparents and check whether they are willing to contribute. Even saving small sums of $50 - $100 per child per month would create a starting point.

1. Andrea's budget

Andrea is a 31-year-old millennial living in Austin, Texas. "Five years ago, I had nothing," she remembers. Years of partying in her early 20s left her with no money, no support system, and no goals for her future.

While she was at college and even after she graduated, she frequently went partying, drinking too much and spending recklessly. She remembers, "when I first started making money, I wasn't sober yet. I would be spending hundreds of dollars out all the time."

Andrea earns a base salary of $20k, but has been increasing her earnings every year, and currently makes another $100k - $120k from commissions in her sales job with a hosting company. Andrea lives alone in a 1-bed apartment. Her company matches up to 3% of salary into her 401K.

Andrea's goals

- Buy a 3-bed house this year for $350K with a $20k deposit.
- Buy a larger duplex property in 3 years and rent out the first property
- Take lavish vacations
- Help family and make charitable donations
- Keep a minimum emergency fund of $15k

Assets

- Savings: $20k
- Deposit for a house; $18k
- 401K: $30k

Andrea's Budget

INCOME			EXPENSES						SUMMARY	
		HOUSEHOLD		CHILDREN		PERSONAL				
ITEM	AMOUNT	ITEM	AMOUNT	NAME	AMOUNT	ITEM	AMOUNT			
Salary 1 (net)	$2,250.00	Rent	$850.00	Clothes	$30.00	Clothes	$30.00		INCOME	$2,250.00
401k (5%+match)		Local taxes	$25.00	Shoes	$15.00	Shoes	$15.00			
Health (Covered)		Electric	$50.00	Childcare		Grooming	$15.00		EXPENSES	$2,200.00
		Water	$40.00	School		Mobile x 2	$60.00			
		Gas Utility		Lunches		gifts	$10.00			
		Phone		pocket money						
		Cable / internet	$40.00	Christmas	$30.00	Entertainment			NET CASH IN / OUT	$50.00
		Misc taxes		Birthdays	$20.00	Sundry cash	$100.00			
		Groceries	$550.00	Sports / clubs		Loans / hp			SAVINGS	$50.00
		Pharmacies	$50.00	Buses / transport		Dry cleaning				
		Gas / petrol	$80.00	Other childcare		Lunches				
		Pets	$10.00			Dining out	$100.00		FLOAT CARRIED FORWARD	$0.00
		Car / van finance				Takeouts				
		Other HP loans				Other transport			OPENING SAVINGS BALANCE	$2,000.00
		Car / van servicing	$40.00							
		Car insurance	$40.00							
		Life insurance							CLOSING SAVINGS BALANCE	$2,050.00

Andrea has a good balance between saving into her 401K and building some property investments, she also takes a prudent attitude towards maintaining an emergency fund. However, with relatively high fixed expenses, in rent and loan repayments, she should ensure that she keeps this at around $20k. She may want to accelerate paying off her student loans to bring this down.

As I mentioned in the outset of this chapter, adopting the practice of budgeting is one of the key ways in which you can improve the way you manage your money, which will consequently enable you to achieve financial success. It may seem like a boring and unnecessary chore, but the benefits that you will reap from implementing a budget are worth the effort. By taking a few hours to create a realistic and achievable budget, you can implement a complete makeover in your financial life. Given that most of your basic expenses are recurrent, making subsequent monthly budgets is going to be super easy and quick once you create the initial one (unless you go the ZBB route). I, therefore, implore you to take the time to analyze your income and expenses and create a 'prototype' budget that will act as a blueprint for future ones.

In conclusion, here are some of the points to remember from this chapter:

- Budgeting involves balancing your income according to your expenses in order to account for your spending more effectively
- Creating a budget allows you to put your finances in order, so as to meet all your goals without increasing liabilities such as debt
- Although making a budget is a simple process that takes a few hours, it can completely transform your financial life and put you on the path to success.

- Start now by gathering together all the information you will need to create your budget.

CHAPTER SEVEN: YOUR FINANCIAL MAKEOVER PLAN

Having a budget to work with can help improve your financial discipline and reduce unnecessary spending. However, physically creating the budget can be primarily mechanical, based on your historical patterns of behavior. For the budget to work and to give you a *financial makeover*, it needs to be personalized in order to be compatible with your goals. In this chapter, we are going to discuss strategies for how you can manage your budget and tailor it to align with your objectives.

Make Sure You Understand Your Goals

When we consider the process of making your budget work to realize your goals, what we are doing is ranking and prioritizing your objectives. Without setting clear goals, it is impossible to grow or progress in your career, personal relationships, or any other aspect of your life.

Now that you have a good grasp on the importance of goals, the question that you may be grappling with is *"How do I figure out what I want in my life?"*. Granted, this question doesn't have a simple answer. After all, our desires and priorities are always in a state of constant change in response to the circumstances that we find ourselves in at any given moment in time. This means what you want today may not necessarily be what you want a year or two from now. Nevertheless, there are several strategies that can help determine the right financial goals to pursue.

If you live with your partner or have children, you should make sure that your financial goals are compatible. This means taking the time to discuss your individual goals and seeking ways of harmonizing them to create shared objectives, which you can jointly work towards. Some of the shared goals that you can create with your partner include, purchasing a property, having children, paying off debts such as student loans and mortgages, establishing a business, saving for retirement, et cetera. Whatever your goals are, it is vital to ensure that you are both on the same page since this will make budgeting easier and more effective.

The Path to Wealth – getting organized.

- Do you want to retire early, or even just ensure you can retire at all?
- Do you want to save towards some specific event, or just build wealth?

You may have heard of the 50/30/20 rule, as it has been around for a while. According to the rule, you should budget 50% of your post-tax income for "needs", 30% for "wants", and 20% for savings and investments. Having said that we are going to throw it all out of the window!

1. First, it's not a rule – it's a very loose guideline.

2. Only a small number of readers will have a 50 / 30/ 20 split as an ideal budget.

The reason we are considering it is to use the broad concept of splitting your budget between these categories. I think that is the really useful part that will give you some structure and a way to test your budget.

Let's move on to discuss and define these categories.

Investments and Savings

This category is the easiest to define because it includes anything you are not spending. This will include, but is not necessarily limited to:

- Rainy day money – emergency funds
- (Early) debt repayments
- Pension savings (401k or SIPP or similar plan)
- Savings for specific events (weddings, babies, extra big vacations)
- Other Investments - in property, stock, shares or bonds

Please note the order of the above list. This is the priority in which it should be tackled; save rainy day money first, and make investing the lowest priority in this category.

Things that you should not include - but you may be tempted - include normal vacations that you go on every year, savings for events (for example, Christmas and birthdays), or any other annualized bills (e.g. car insurance). These should all be included in needs or wants.

The title of this section was the path to wealth for a good reason. I am assuming that you are reading this book because you have some financial goals you want to achieve. Therefore, decide how much you are going to allocate to this category first - the amount will depend on the scale of your goals.

If you are struggling financially on a low wage, don't try to be too ambitious with this category. Try and make it at least 10%.

At the other end of the spectrum, if you are young, earning a good wage without many commitments, then make this high (the higher the better. It could be 50% or even more).

The mid-ground for a middle-income family is going to be in the range of 15% to 25%. Be as ambitious as you can to build wealth faster. Ensure that you make these savings/payments as soon as you receive your income to ensure that you deliver your key goals and work with what is left. We call this paying yourself first.

Needs

This category includes everything that you can't live without. This would normally include the following categories:

- Housing: rent or mortgage and associated taxes
- Utility bills
- Insurance including health and life
- Groceries and pharmacies
- Minimum debt repayments

At first glance, this category appears really easy to define, but you are going to find that it is not as straightforward as it seems, especially if you have to negotiate this with a partner.

If we are strict about this, there is very little that we cannot live without except the most meager of shelter and food. It wasn't so long ago that a whole family, including parents, would be crowded into a one-room tenement.

However, that is not likely to be considered a satisfactory minimum for most of us!

The reality is that you can put anything in here that you define as necessary. Mobile phone? 6 bedroom house? Car? Is cable a utility?

Ultimately it's up to you to decide what to include, but the more you put into here then, the less flexibility you are going to have with your wants.

The ultimate point of the exercise is to see how much you have left for "wants", and how you are going to split it. As an indicator, you are looking at 50%, but it could be much higher or lower, depending on your circumstances. For instance, it will be lower for young adults who have few fixed commitments but higher for young families.

Wants

Wants are every other type of spend that you haven't put into needs. This typically includes;

- Clothes - most clothes spending is discretionary (i.e. we tend to buy more or better quality than the minimum necessary to keep us from freezing or from getting us arrested if we go out).
- Phones
- Restaurants/going out
- Entertainment – cable, Netflix, Spotify, etc.
- Vacations
- Gifts: Birthdays and Christmas
- Car?

Whichever category you put "car" into, you should also put the associated tax, insurance, and servicing costs.

In the end, "wants" will be the money that you have left

to work with after your investments and needs categories have been taken care of. This is where the interesting decisions and discussions start and ultimately, where the hard choices will need to be made.

How to calculate the split.

For you to see how the split between these three categories works, you have to add up all your post-tax income from your pay stubs. You will have to add back any deductions for pension or health to the net amount you receive each month/week. Then take the total for each category (i.e. savings / needs / wants) and divide by your post tax income then multiply by 100.

E.g. Total Wants / Net income x 100 = % spent on wants

If you haven't budgeted for all items every month, then you must annualize all the numbers (i.e. take the monthly post tax income and multiply by 12). For example, if you don't have a monthly budget for gifts that allows for all birthdays, Christmas, and so on, then you need to work out your income and all expenditure on an annual basis (annualized). However, if you have taken the costs of gifts over the entire year and divided by 12 to get a monthly amount, and you have done that consistently for all categories of expense, then you can use a monthly income.

I have produced a personal finance calculator that will be invaluable as an aid to setting a budget and working this out. You can get it for free by clicking on the link.

To achieve your financial goals, you must master the art of making difficult financial choices and prioritizing those that are going to contribute most towards them. This will help to avoid continuous drift and periodic setbacks. By setting a budget and understanding how it splits between needs, wants and savings, you help crystalize these choices. Moreover, once you prioritize saving and investments, you will get the best chance of successfully achieving your goals and aims.

Why you need to keep rainy day money set aside

There are two components that you should set aside as 'rainy day' money. The first component of the rainy day money is a Murphy fund (after Murphy's law - if it can go wrong, it will go wrong). This refers to money that you set aside to help you cover short-term expenses that may arise in the month. For instance, you may experience an unplanned dental issue that requires you to consult a dentist or a sudden breakdown of your car, which requires immediate repairs.

So, the Murphy fund is meant to help you cater for these relatively small unplanned expenses and keep you afloat until your next paycheck arrives. This ensures that you don't need to take an overdraft - *which could interfere with your budget*. Many calls on your Murphy fund can be foreseen in some ways. If your fridge is fifteen years old and making strange noises, it won't be a huge surprise when it 'suddenly' stops working.

The second component is an emergency fund, in that it allows you to prepare for serious and unexpected events that may require you to spend money that you hadn't anticipated. However, the main difference between the two is that in contrast, while a Murphy fund is meant for smaller one-off expenses, an emergency fund cushions you against major events such as sudden job loss or serious medical emergencies. In case you are laid off from your job, for example, your emergency fund should be able to help you cater for your expenses and stay afloat for a certain period of time as you look for new employment or source of income.

Putting a percentage of your income into Murphy funds and emergency funds can be very advantageous for a number of reasons, including:

- It provides you with a financial safety net, thus reducing the stress of having to deal with unplanned events.
- It helps you to develop a saving mindset since you are less likely to spend money extravagantly if you are preparing for the future
- It prevents you from dipping into other savings accounts in case of emergencies, thus allowing you to stay on track with your financial targets
- It helps you avoid taking on unnecessary debt in case of emergencies, thus providing you with greater control over your financial decisions.

It is worth noting that rainy day money is very different from investment money. While the former is specifically designed to cover unexpected expenses and emergencies that may arise in the future, the latter helps to facilitate income-generating opportunities.

How Much Should You Keep in Rainy Day Money?

Since a Murphy fund is meant to cover smaller, unplanned expenses that arise during the month, you don't need to put a lot of money into it like you would with an emergency fund. For instance, you can set your target to be between $1,000 and $3,000. This is because you are unlikely to need more than that to pay for a short-term expense. It is always best to start small and gradually increase the amount you put into it whenever possible. A good place to start would be to put any loose change, or one dollar bills that you get back after shopping into a penny jar. This might seem very inconsequential at first, but as you develop this habit, you will begin to notice your rainy day savings increasing.

When it comes to an emergency fund, many experts recommend that you should save enough money to cover 3 - 6 months of your living expenses. This includes your fixed costs such as rent or mortgage payments and credit card payments as well as variable costs such as groceries, entertainment, gas, and utilities. The reason for the 3 to 6 months of expense rule is because most major emergencies can take longer to resolve, and during that time, you need to have a means of meeting your living expenses all the same. For example, if you get fired from your job, it can take several months of job hunting before you secure another one. During this interim period, your emergency fund will enable you to continue covering your expenses, thus providing you with a safety net and protecting you from a financial crisis *(at least for a period of time)*

Where Should You Keep Your Rainy Day Money?

It is important to keep your rainy-day funds separate from other savings such as investment funds. This makes it easier for you to track your savings and prevent the temptation of using the fund for something that it was not intended.

A savings account is more appropriate for saving Murphy money as it provides you with liquidity, which means you can conveniently access and withdraw your money in cash if you need to use it to pay for an unplanned expense. Savings accounts generally earn lower interest, so you won't be able to make much out of it in terms of increasing your savings -

however, you should be able to access them immediately. The main goal of putting your Murphy fund in a savings account is to avoid using it on other things.

In contrast, a money market account is a direct deposit account that pays interest according to the current rates in the market. In general, the interest rates for money market accounts tend to be higher than those offered with savings accounts. You will only need to have a high minimum balance to earn high interest on these accounts, and sometimes, they can be a little more inconvenient or take longer to access.

Since major emergencies that can destabilize your budget are pretty rare occurrences, you may end up going an entire year or more without even touching your emergency funds. By depositing your emergency funds in a money market account, therefore, you are able to increase your balance, or in other words, make your money work for you.

Saving vs. Paying Off Debt - Which Should You Prioritize?

Saving and paying off your debt are arguably the two most important prerequisites that you need to do before you can achieve financial freedom. However, with limited income and plenty of living expenses to cover every month, it can be challenging to decide on which of these two you should focus on.

So, should you start putting money into your retirement savings or should you focus on paying your creditors and becoming debt-free?

Well, you may remember the table in chapter 5, which showed the difference between running a $100 per month deficit versus the same surplus. How the debtor ended up owing over $12000, and the investor had a pot of $8000. Because investment returns are uncertain, and due to the high rates of interest (and it always accrues), it is usually best to pay off debt.

Once you have your Murphy fund, concentrate on paying off all your debt except your mortgage and perhaps vehicle and federal student loans. Thereafter, build your emergency funds. Once these have reached 3 months' worth of income, it is prudent to start splitting the money into investment funds while completing your emergency fund. However, fully clear any student loans before investing.

One exception to this would be if your company matches your pension contribution. This is free money (100% return), and you should *always* take full advantage up to the maximum allowed.

Why You Should Prioritize Paying Off Debt

The primary reason to prioritize debt repayment is the unseen damage it is doing to your financial future. Those interest payments have a double negative effect. Firstly, they are eating your cash flow now, which will hinder your current situation. Secondly, you are not investing that cash flow into wealth-generating assets that will give you a financially prosperous future.

Remember, bad debts are those that drain your income, are unaffordable, and do not offer any long term value. Bad debts generally lack realistic repayment plans since they do not generate income. A good example of bad debt is taking a loan to go on a luxury holiday that you are unable to afford. Of course, there is nothing inherently wrong with going on holiday if you can afford it. However, there is no point taking a loan to go on a holiday for a few weeks only to spend years of your life repaying it. If you need to take out a loan to go on holiday, it means you cannot afford it.

Another bad debt would be charging your credit card to buy an expensive TV. Again, it is normal to desire a huge 60-inch flat-screen TV in your living room. However, if you cannot afford to pay for it in cash, it would be foolhardy to incur debt so that you can own it. After all, a TV set is a depreciating asset that begins to lose value as soon as you take it out of the store. It also does nothing to increase your income, which could mean there is no realistic way of repaying back the debt unless you take on another debt to pay it back.

Regularly taking on bad debts, including "interest-free" loans, can put you in a vicious cycle of borrowing, which will eventually put a strain on your income and make it harder for you to achieve your goals. However, the negative effects of bad debt are not only limited to your finances. When your debts accumulate and become more difficult to pay back, the pressure can take a toll on your professional life, relationships, and mental health.

Here are some of the reasons why you should make debt payment a top priority when budgeting.

- Enables You to Have More Free Income

If you are overburdened by debt, you end up losing a huge chunk of your income to repay not only the principal but the interest that accumulates monthly or annually. The longer you are stuck repaying the debt, the more you end up paying as the interest continues to pile. On the other hand, if you can find a way of repaying your outstanding debts sooner, you end up paying less interest, thus saving money in the long run.

- Allows You to Reduce Risk

Having lots of debt puts you at a significantly higher financial risk than you would ordinarily be in without debt. If you are already drowning in debt and don't have an emergency fund to cushion yourself, you are always one financial blow away from catastrophe. If you lose your job or suffer a medical emergency, you may end up not being able to pay your debt, which can lead to a lot of problems including:

- Being constant hounded by creditors

- Getting your car repossessed

- Losing your home through foreclosure since you can no longer pay your mortgage

Clearing your debt early helps you to free your income so that you can budget without constantly worrying about unexpected events ruining your life.

- Improves Your Credit Score

Having a good credit score is very advantageous as it makes it easier to secure loans at fair interest rates. However, your credit score is largely dependent on how well you handle your debts. If you have a lot of debt that you are unable to repay or frequently default on paying, your credit rating will reduce, thus making it difficult for you to secure more credit. Even if you manage to find institutions that are willing to advance more credit, you will likely be charged very high-interest rates since creditors perceive you to be a high-risk debt. On the flip side, paying your debts on time will improve your credit score and make it easy for you to procure loans (mortgages) at good interest rates.

- Relieves You of Stress

Being in debt can be a major stressor in life. You end up constantly worrying about how you will meet all your living expenses and dreading what could happen if you lose your job. The relentless pressure of working to pay back your debt and the feeling of guilt whenever you spend on simple pleasures can take a toll on your mental health and peace of mind. Clearing your debt as soon as possible will relieve you of this unnecessary pressure and declutter your mind of stressful thoughts, thus allowing you to focus your time and energy in more productive pursuits.

- Allows You to Invest in the Future

Paying off your debt early enables you to invest in the future. With the weight of debt lifted off your shoulders, you can focus on saving money for retirement, invest in your kids' education or put down a deposit on a home so that you can become a homeowner.

- Improves Your Self Esteem

If you are constantly drowning in debt, your self-esteem may suffer greatly as a result. In an effort to hide your struggling financial situation from family and friends, you may end up going out of your way to 'create' an impression of a perfect life by buying new clothes, an expensive new phone, or even a brand new car. Since all of these require money, you are likely to take on more debt, thus sinking yourself even deeper in debt. On the other hand, paying off your debt can improve your confidence and eliminate anxiety since you won't have any reason to hide your financial situation from your close friends and family members.

Which Debts Should You Prioritize and Why?

If you are overwhelmed with debt, it can be challenging to decide which debts to deal with first. Generally, there are two main approaches to debt payment. On the one hand, you can choose to settle the debts from the highest interest rates to the lowest. This allows you to cut down on high interest and save money in the long run. Alternatively, you may decide to pay off the debts starting from the smallest to the largest. This helps you to gather momentum in your debt repayment plan and clear your debt much faster. Let us look at both of these strategies to see how they work and why you may opt for one over the other.

- Paying High-Interest Debts First

Choosing to pay off high-interest debt first makes a lot of sense because this debt costs you the most money every month. By prioritizing this debt first, you can significantly cut down on the amount of interest you pay and free up money which you can use to service other debts. This debt repayment plan, however, has a downside in the sense that if your debt with the highest interest rate is also your largest debt, you may spend a very long time paying it. This can make you feel like you are not making much progress in your debt repayment, which can be discouraging. As a result, you may find it harder to remain focussed on your debt repayment plan.

- Paying the Smaller Debt First

Paying your smaller debts first can be a very satisfying approach to use in debt repayment. This is because you can clear your small debts much quicker. This can give you a boost in confidence and make you feel like you are making progress, which will motivate you to tackle your more sizable debts. The drawback of this debt-repayment strategy, however, is that you end up paying higher interest on your larger debts, and this means you will end up paying a lot of interest in the long run.

As you can see, each of these debt repayment strategies has its advantages as well as its downsides. Therefore, when creating a repayment plan for clearing your debt, you should select a balanced strategy that works best for you, and one that allows you to achieve your financial goals much quicker. With a balanced approach, you can knock out all your debts in the shortest amount of time and get back on track with your financial objectives.

If you have small debts that you can clear quickly, you should focus on settling those first and then decide whether you will pay off the remaining debt according to the interest rate or total amount of debt. Always settle payday loans as fast as possible due to the astronomical interest rates they charge. Usually, these loans are quite small, so you would treat them first under both methods. In case you have different credit card debts with the same interest rate, you can choose to settle the smallest balance first before servicing those with higher balances. Regardless of the strategy that you employ to service your debts, it is crucial that you stick with the plan. This means channeling any extra cash towards your debts to clear them much faster. You may also want to increase your monthly payments to chip off your larger debts, such as mortgages, in the shortest amount of time. Normally under either method, your mortgage and vehicle loans would be among the last to be settled because they are both larger and lower interest rates.

It is very critical that you remain motivated as you implement your debt repayment plan; otherwise, you risk falling off the horse and defaulting on payments, which can lead to an accumulation of interest. One of the best ways to remain focussed on your debt repayment is to create a debt payment chart to keep track of your progress. This will help you to determine whether your strategy is working or it requires some modifications. Finally, remember to celebrate any milestones that you achieve along the way.

In conclusion, here are some of the key points to remember from this chapter:

The Priority of Action Steps to Achieve Financial Independence
1. Build a Murphy fund of $1000 - $3000
2. Pay off higher-interest deb
3. Build an emergency fund of 3 to 6 months of expenses
4. Build investment assets
5. Pay off lower-interest debt such as mortgage (steps 4 and 5 can run in parallel).

- A budget is an essential financial tool that can help reduce your spending and better organize your income
- Set your investment goals and allocate this money first, then see to needs and what is left goes to "wants".
- Clearing your debt should be a top priority in your budget as it enables you to create more

income, increase your credit score and achieve peace of mind
- You should always be consistent in your debt repayment plan to prevent the accumulation of interest and cut down on your debt faster

In the next chapter, we are going to look at how you can reduce your spending and pay off your outstanding debts.

CHAPTER EIGHT: HOW TO CUT YOUR SPENDING AND PRIORITIZE OTHER GOALS

Reducing your spending is crucial if you hope to get rid of debt and increase your income. By cutting down on your expenses and working with a budget, you can create surplus income to service your debt and ease the financial pressure that may be weighing you down.

One of the challenges of this process is always how to maximize your cash flow. So, in this chapter, we are going to look at some of the ways you can shave off unnecessary expenses from your budget and free up money to pursue your financial goals.

Zero Based Budgeting

Zero-based budgeting (ZBB) is a way of budgeting your money from scratch each month, such that your total income minus your expenses comes to zero. It is one of the most effective ways to squeeze spending/ It will mean that all your expense categories start from zero each month, you must justify every expense before allocating it to a particular expense in your budget. For example, if your income is

$2000 per month, all of your expenses, savings, and debt payments should add up to $2000. The zero-based budget enables you to plan your money in a manner that guarantees every penny is accounted for, and that every dollar that you earn is working as hard as possible.

Some of the advantages of zero-based budgeting include:

- It guarantees efficient allocation of money according to needs and benefits, thus helping to avoid unnecessary spending
- It helps to weed out counterproductive expenses
- It forces one to account for all their spending thus instilling financial discipline
- The main benefit is that it forces you to discuss and agree to all financial expenditure with your partner every month, which helps to ensure you stay on the same page and are both committed to the goals.

The ZBB method, however, has some downsides. These include:

- Requires a lot of commitment to implement properly
- It may not be possible or practical to justify every expense

Although a zero-based budget requires a lot of dedication during implementation, it can be very effective in helping to curb unnecessary spending. You should try to incorporate this method into your budgeting practice if you are seeking to cut down your expenditure as much as possible.

21 Ways to Cut Your Spending

It is important to limit your spending as much as possible when preparing your budget. Failure to curb overspending is likely to strain your finances and keep you stuck living paycheck to paycheck. This can make it much harder to stick to your budget and possibly keep you chained to a cycle of debt, since you may end up borrowing more to furnish your lifestyle. So, how exactly can you regulate your spending to achieve the surplus that you need? Well, here are some of the ways you can cut down on your spending in different areas and free up more money in your budget

- Walk or Cycle (to Work) Whenever Possible

Obviously, if you work dozens of miles away from your residence, your only option may be to commute either using public means or your own private vehicle. However, if your place of work is not far from where you live, walking or cycling to work may be the best way to go. This will not only help you to cut down on fares and fuel costs but also provide an opportunity to keep fit and healthy. So it's ultimately a win-win situation for you.

- Carpool

If you have neighbors who commute to work, you can save a lot of money by carpooling. Sharing a ride with others allows you to split the cost of the commute, which means you will end up paying less compared to what you would have paid while traveling by yourself.

- Use Public Transportation

Another great way to cut down on transport costs if you work away from home is to use public means of transportation. Commuting via public transports saves you money on gas, car maintenance, and parking fees.

If you can remove one vehicle altogether from family ownership then large savings await!

- Switch to a Cash-only System

Adopting a cash-only spending policy is a very effective way of controlling your spending when you go shopping. This is mainly due to the fact that when you spend cash, you get the visceral experience of seeing your money running out. Spending cash can, therefore, can force you to live within your means and minimize debt. If you decide to employ this cash-only approach to budgeting and spending, you can set automated payments for your essentials such as rent and utilities and then restrict your spending to the remaining cash.

- Establish a 48-hour Rule for Purchases

One of the best ways to curb compulsive spending habits and cut down on expenses is by consciously delaying purchases. By instituting a 48-hour rule before purchasing products, you give yourself time to think whether the purchase is worthwhile. This will not only help you to restrict your spending habits but also minimize buyer's remorse.

- Buy the cheapest item.

This may seem self-evident, but we have been conditioned by the psychological influencers that more expensive must be better. However, this is now exploited by shops and brands to our detriment, who put out more expensive products just to entice us to pick the mid-priced option.

We believe the motto *"buy cheap, buy twice"*. Just ensure

that this is true before acting.

- Keep a Penny Jar

In addition to having a savings allocation in your budget, you should always keep a penny jar in your house where you can put loose change whenever you shop. Open up the jar every end of the month or every few months to see how much you have. You may be very surprised to find out just how much money you can end up collecting from this simple DIY saving plan.

A more 21st-century method would be to use an app, or card (e.g. moneybox.com) that will do this for you, so that every time you spend it will round the amount up, and sweep the rounded amount to a savings account.

- How to Cut Spending on Clothes

Avoid fashion shopping. Fashion is designed to change with every season and every year. Look for quality items of clothing that are classic and never go out of fashion, and ones that can be mixed and matched.

- Shop in Thrift Shops Whenever Possible

You can cut down significantly on the amount of money you spend on clothing by shopping in thrift stores at least some of the time. Most of these shops tend to stock up on high-quality designer wear and one-off clothing pieces, which you can get for next to nothing. So, the next time you feel the need to upgrade your wardrobe, be sure to check the affordable options first.

- Plan your meals in advance and shop from a list

Grocery spend is often a big part of the household budget. Ideally, you should make a list of the quantities and ingredients that you will need for the week, based on a meal plan. Thereafter, use this to build your shopping list so that you only buy what you will need.

- Ready meals

Ready meals are very convenient for the time-poor. However, the cost of ready meals adds substantial amounts to your grocery bills. Look up simple, fast recipes and cook from scratch. They will also be more healthy, in all probability, without added salt and trans-fat.

- Purchase Unbranded Products when Shopping in the Supermarket

In most cases, there is very little difference between branded and unbranded food products when it comes to quality and taste. So, instead of spending extra for canned tomatoes with attractive packaging, why not purchase the cheaper unbranded alternative, which probably tastes just as good? You will get to save some extra coins, which will help to free up your budget. Saving a few cents on every item in your cart really does add up, especially over weeks and months.

- Cook Your Meals in Bulk

Bulk cooking your meals is a great way of cutting down on food expenses, because you can buy items in larger quantities which is often cheaper. Simply set aside some time during the weekend to prepare a variety of dishes that can take you through the entire week and store them in the freezer. This will help minimize the tendency of ordering takeout meals - *which can be very expensive in some cases.*

- Look out for supermarket loyalty schemes.

Many supermarkets run loyalty schemes. These can either give you some form of cashback, or they may give you extra savings on their own brands.

- Always Switch off Lights & Devices Whenever You are not Using them.

Electricity is one of the utilities that use up a chunk of most people's expenses. If you have several electronic gadgets running constantly, your power bills are likely to stack up. One of the ways you can minimize spending on power is by switching off your lights and other electrical devices whenever you are not using them or when you are away. This will help to conserve power, thus reducing your monthly electricity bills. Items left in standby mode still consume power and can be switched off entirely.

- Invest in Energy Saving Bulbs

If you've noticed that you tend to spend a lot on electricity, another way you can cut down on your power bills is by replacing your traditional halogen or filament bulbs with energy-saving LED or incandescent bulbs. Although you may have to pay more for these units, they can significantly reduce your power consumption, thus saving you a lot of money in the long run. Furthermore, energy-efficient bulbs tend to last much longer than filament bulbs, so you won't need to replace them very often.

- Cut down on Heating and Aircon

More effective than changing to energy-saving bulbs would be to cut your heating by a couple of degrees. This doesn't make too much difference to the comfort but has an exponential effect on the energy consumed. Likewise, turn the air-con down by setting to a higher temperature.

- Cut out Mid-week drinking.

The cost of alcohol adds up, whether you drink at home or especially if you go out. Keep drinking for the weekend, and you will improve your health too.

- Find Activities that Don't Cost Money

If you often spend a huge chunk of your income on entertainment, you can greatly reduce this expense by finding alternatives that are fun and free. For example, if you love going out with friends and often end up spending too much on food and drinks, you can cut down on this cost by planning home cook-outs where you can still catch up and have fun without spending too much. Similarly, if you enjoy going to concerts because of the music and the crowds, you can find free concerts in your locality where you will be able to have the same experience without spending a lot.

There are plenty of fun activities which you can take part in without having to spend any money. These include:

- Going to the park for a picnic
- Reading books at the local library
- Visiting a local museum
- Playing board games
- Hiking

- Taking part in community sports tournaments
- Having a yard sale
- Volunteering at a community center

No Spend Challenge

A no-spend challenge is a highly effective way of resetting your budget and cutting down on your spending to create surplus income. It mainly involves challenging yourself to not spend any money on anything apart from basic essentials over a given duration of time. This could be a weekend, a week, or even a month. If you find yourself constantly making trips to the store and overspending on non-essential items, a no-spend challenge can help control your impulses and restore sanity in your spending habits.

So, how does the no spend challenge work?

Basically, you need to set your own rules and then make sure that your credit and debit cards are safely locked up somewhere you can't access easily. While the rules can vary from person to person *(depending on their unique needs)*, the idea is to spend only on needs and not wants. Whether an item qualifies as a need or want is something that you will have to decide yourself.

Some of the items that you are allowed to spend on during no spend challenge may include:

- Utilities
- Rent or Mortgage
- Internet and phone bills
- Groceries
- Fuel
- Insurance

Here are some of the items you can choose to cut down on during your no-spend challenge:

- Recreational activities which cost money
- Eating out/ drinks
- Clothes
- Uber/taxi expenses
- Anything else that is not an essential need

There are several tips that can help you to succeed in your no-spend challenge. These include:

i) Have an Objective in Mind

Before you even start making the rules for your no spend challenge, you need to understand why exactly you are doing it. For instance, is your goal to speed up debt repayment? Are you trying to save up for retirement? Do you want to save money for a new investment opportunity? Having a clear goal in mind will provide you with the motivation to follow through with the no spend challenge that you have set for yourself.

ii) Decide on a Time Frame

The longer you are able to follow through with the no spend challenge, the greater the reward. While it may not be possible to avoid spending for an entire month, you will be able to save a lot more if you stick to the challenge for as long as possible. Perhaps you can start with a week of no spending and gauge your progress before deciding whether to extend the duration.

iii) Set Simple Rules

You need to come up with your own set of rules on what you are willing and able to cut out of your spending. It is important that you evaluate yourself honestly when gauging what you are able to do without in your budget. While you want rules that are serious enough to motivate you to act, they shouldn't be so draconian that you end up bailing on the challenge only a few days later.

iv) Share Your Plan with Others

Earlier on, we discussed the benefits of making a public commitment and how it can inspire you to effect positive change in your spending habits. By sharing your resolution with your friends and family, you will get the motivation and support that will help you to succeed in your challenge.

You can also put up your no spend challenge on your Facebook or Instagram and encourage your followers to join you. This will make the challenge a lot more interactive and fun.

Participating in a no-spend challenge is undoubtedly a great opportunity to reboot your budget and create surplus income, which you can use to improve your financial prospects. There are countless success stories of people who have managed to completely rejuvenate their financial lives simply by applying this strategy. To illustrate the power of this strategy, let us examine the story of a client that I worked with a few years ago who we will call Frank.

After spending hundreds of dollars to plan his graduation party, Frank realized that he had suddenly hit rock bottom financially. Although he had managed to secure a job as a research analyst at a local company, his salary was hardly enough to sustain the party lifestyle that he had become so accustomed to. With over $30,000 in student loans to repay, Frank understood that simply making a budget wouldn't be enough to get him out of the financial rut that he found himself in. More drastic measures needed to be undertaken. So he decided that he was not going to spend any money for six months, with the only exceptions being essential expenses such as rent, groceries, and utility bills. He resolved not to spend any money on online shopping sprees, night-out parties and to cut down on the number of times he ordered take out. Within 6 months, he had saved up enough money to pay back a quarter of his debt while living on an income of $56,000. Frank's success with the no spend challenge was so remarkable, and he actually enjoyed the process, that he decided to make it a regular part of his financial strategy.

Just like Frank and many others who have been successful with the no spend challenge, you too can derive great benefit in cutting down your spending using this method. While it may seem like an extreme way of managing your spending habits, you can significantly increase your surplus income through the no spend challenge and put yourself on the path to financial success.

In summary, here are the key takeaways from this chapter:

- By cutting your spending, you can drastically reduce your debt and improve your financial position
- The no-spend challenge is a great way to motivate yourself to spend less and save more
- Minimizing your expenses will empower you to budget more effectively so that you can create surplus income to meet your financial goals.

CHAPTER NINE: PLAN FOR LIFE

So far, we have discussed the importance of having a monthly budget as part of your financial strategy and how you can use this to give yourself a financial makeover. We have also looked at how to create a working budget and cut down on your expenses to generate extra income to ensure that your budget is working for you. In this chapter, we are going to discuss how you can manage your budget on an ongoing basis, and some of the benefits you will derive from doing so.

Why You Need to Maintain and Regularly Adjust Your Budget

Creating and maintaining a budget is a very crucial part of finance management. By developing a budget and adhering to it, you can ensure that you always have money to cater to your needs and things that are important to you. For instance, you can determine how much you need to spend on essentials like groceries, rent, and utilities, as well as any desires you may have, such as going on vacation, buying a new TV, and so on. In addition to this, planning your spending through a budget enables you to live within your means, thus keeping you from accumulating debt and clearing off any debt that you may already have.

Although creating a budget is pretty simple, most people find it hard to stick to a budget and manage it on an ongoing basis. It is important to realize that a budget is a constantly evolving business. So, you need to regularly adjust it as you collect new information about your spending and income. One of the best ways to keep track of your finances through a budget is to map out your spending for 6 months to one year down the road. This allows you to predict months where your spending may be higher or lower than expected. Consequently, you will be able to find ways of balancing out the highs and lows in your budget. For instance, if you have a major expense coming up in 6 months, you can tweak your budget by cutting down on some recurrent expenditures in areas such as entertainment and clothes to free up money, which you can then use to cover the expense when the time comes. In doing so, you will be able to balance your spending such that you are able to clear the non-recurring expense without really blowing up your budget or taking on more debt.

Another benefit of extending your budget into the future is that it allows you to forecast how much you will be able to save for long-term financial goals that are important to you. For example, you may be planning to buy a newer car or renovate your home in a few months. By updating your budget to account for this future expense, you can plan your income wisely to save the money that you need to meet these objectives.

Review your goals

As we discussed in chapter 4, it is important that you review your goals regularly. If your goals change or adapt, and that is quite likely, then your budget will also need to change and adapt. You should review all your major goals once per quarter, or at least bi-annually. Take some time out to do this and go somewhere neutral with your partner, like a coffee shop. Smaller goals and your budget should be tracked more often, at least once per week, possibly every day.

How to Ensure Savings are Savings

When creating a budget, it is very important to allocate a percentage of your income to savings. It is not uncommon for people to underestimate the value of savings. Most individuals tend to view saving as being at the bottom of the priority list when budgeting. It is not surprising then that people who don't prioritize saving often end up broke as soon as they receive their paychecks.

Unless you make it your priority to save part of your income, you may find it difficult to get out of the cycle of living paycheck to paycheck, and most likely never achieve any of your financial goals. Be that as it may, saving is not always an easy thing to do. Setting aside a portion of your income can be very challenging, especially if you have plenty of living expenses to cover and debt to pay.

However, there are a number of strategies that you can employ to start saving and ensure that your savings are not used for any other purpose. These include:

- Make Saving Fixed Item in Your Budget

When preparing a monthly budget, set a target for savings, and then make your budget deliver to this target by cutting expenditure on "wants", where necessary. If possible, ensure that regular investment amounts are set aside like an expense.you should include savings in your list of expenses. By doing this, you are less likely to be tempted to spend the money on something else.

- Have a Specific Account for Savings

Instead of keeping savings in your checking account, you need to have a different account, where you specifically deposit funds that you intend to save. I would highly recommend setting an automatic transfer so that a percentage of your income is directly transferred to your savings account *(automatically)* every month. This will ensure that you meet your monthly savings target every month without fail.

- Use a Sweeper Function on Bank Accounts to Transfer 'Excess' to Savings

A sweeper account combines elements of a savings account and fixed deposit account to give you the best of both worlds. The way that this works is that the bank links your savings account to your fixed deposit account. When your set saving limit is attained, any excess cash is directly transferred to the fixed deposit account, thus enabling you to earn higher rates of return. To make use of the sweeper function, you need to decide how much you are willing to keep in your savings account - which is known as the threshold. The amount you choose to save can be 3 to 6 months of your expenses, or any amount that you may require within a short period of time.

Amounts below your threshold limit will be available in your savings account in the form of cash to provide you with liquidity in case you require it on short notice. For example, funds for vacation, emergencies, car replacement, house deposit, etc. Any extra amount is automatically converted to Fixed Deposit, and you will start earning interest from it according to the Fixed Deposit rate set by your bank, while some bank accounts will allow you to have different linked accounts for each type of saving. However, if your bank account doesn't have this function, you can simply track your savings by yourself.

How to Track and Stick to Your Budget - Techniques and Tools

Developing the habit of sticking to your budget is just as important as making the budget. Failure to adhere to your budget can lead to unnecessary or unplanned spending, which will make it harder to save, thus keeping you from accomplishing your goals. On the flip side, if you always try to stick to your budget, it will be easier to meet your financial targets, such as saving and debt payment - which will ultimately improve your financial situation.

Here are key techniques that can help you stick to your budget:

- The Envelope System (Dave Ramsey)

The envelope system is a simple method of tracking your spending and sticking to your budget. You are required to create a budget *(with all of your expenses included)* and put money for each expense in a separate envelope. This means you are only limited to spending money allocated on the envelope.

So, if you tend to go overboard with particular expenses, this strategy can help you to rein in your spending and bring it under control. Here is how to go about it:

i) Decide which Budget Categories Require a Cash Envelope

The cash envelope system is best used for expenses that tend to bust your budget, for example, groceries, gas, entertainment, car maintenance, and personal items. So, you should decide which expenses you are likely to overspend on and make them the candidates for your cash envelope budgeting strategy.

ii) Determine how much You Want to Spend on that Expense

Once you've isolated the items that you tend to overspend on, figure out how much you want to spend on them, and stick with that. Be sure to run this through your partner or spouse so that you are on the same page moving forward. If you are single, consult with your accountability buddy to get their input.

iii) Create Envelopes for each Expense and Fill it With the Budgeted Amount

Suppose you've budgeted $200 for a month's worth of groceries, you should put this cash in the envelope designated for groceries. And when you go shopping, try to stick to this amount and avoid any impulse buying. So, for example, if you take a trip to the store and put things in your cart which exceed this amount, remove some items from your cart and put them back on the shelf so that you don't end up with a deficit. In case you have some remaining cash, put it back in the envelope.

As a rule of thumb, you should only spend what you've put in each cash envelope. If you run out of money for groceries, for example, go check your pantry for anything that you can use to prepare a meal. As tempting as it may be to borrow money from other envelopes, you should resist the urge to do so since this will lead to a deficit in those budget categories.

By becoming more intentional with your budgeting, you will be able to manage your money better and get rid of the tendency to overspend whenever you have money.

- **Prepaid Cards and eWallets**

Prepaid cards are a great way to stick to your budget since they keep you from overspending. Even on rare occasions - *when you end up going over what you have loaded* - these cards usually don't charge overdraft fees, thus making it easier to track your finances. Most prepaid cards also allow you to access mobile management tools to help you budget and set savings targets.

Here are some tips on how you can capitalize on prepaid cards to improve your budgeting and monitor your spending:

- Choose prepaid cards that have convenience features such as eWallets so that you can make purchases using your mobile device
- Ensure your prepaid cards have a wide network of ATMs so that you can access your cash from anywhere. Using ATMs that are out of your network coverage is likely to cost more in transaction charges
- Use your prepaid cards to pay for specific bills and expenses such as utilities, groceries, and gas. This will prevent you from making purchases that you've not budgeted for.

- **Mobile Banking Apps**

Mobile banking apps can be useful when it comes to managing your finances and maintaining a budget. Part of the allure of mobile banking apps is that they provide you with unfettered access to your financial accounts anytime, anywhere. This makes it easy and convenient to track your spending and stick within the limits of your budget. In addition to this, mobile banking apps provide you with greater control over your finances. You are able to deposit funds in your account remotely, which makes it easier and quicker to save money.

Automate everything

It is best to remove as many financial chores as possible from your to-do list. This generally makes life run much more smoothly, and avoid things like charges for late payments. Therefore set up automated payments for credit cards, preferably to pay the full balance, and also all your rent/mortgage and utility bills, plus any local taxes or garbage collection. In addition, make sure that those saving and investment payments also happen automatically.

Adapting Your Budget to Changing Circumstances

A budget is a constantly evolving document that changes according to prevailing circumstances. What works today may not necessarily work tomorrow. For instance, government policy on taxation can impact your budget. If taxes are raised, you may end up earning less than you did before, thus making it necessary to modify your budget appropriately. Similarly, if you suddenly lose your job, you may need to completely overhaul your budget and create a new one that allows you to live within your means *(through savings)* until you get a new job.

In light of these unpredictable changes, it is important to look at your budget regularly *(ideally on a month-to-month basis)* so that you are able to modify your spending habits according to changing circumstances. For example, if there is a sudden increase in prices of certain products, you can opt to swop your suppliers, cut down on how much of the product you purchase, or go for an alternative product, which is cheaper.

By making your budget responsive to changes in circumstances and modifying your spending habits accordingly, you will be able to live within your means and avoid breaking your budget.

In conclusion, here are the key points that you should remember from this chapter:

- A budget is a living document that should be regularly reviewed to make it adaptable to ever-changing situations.
- Review your goals regularly and ensure that your budget is still aligned to meet those goals.
- Automate everything. Start to do this now.
- Prepaid cards offer greater control over finances and can help you to track your spending as well as perform tasks such as saving and paying expenses remotely and conveniently.

CHAPTER TEN: ACHIEVE FINANCIAL PROSPERITY

It is time to get to some of the more advanced elements of your financial makeover that will utilize your financial maturity and to talk about steps that you can take to begin to grow and accelerate your wealth.

It is important to emphasize the investment mindset at this point. The correct amount of investment risk for most people will be low, therefore you should be thinking: *get rich slow*. This is time for long term thinking about how to grow your wealth over the years. There are exceptions if you make a lot of money, and you are younger, then you could adopt a more aggressive strategy. Generally the younger you are the more aggressive you can afford to be. However, I won't cover that here as it would not be right for most people and is a whole topic itself.

When I refer to long term thinking over short term thinking, it is to put aside the notion of taking shortcuts to get rich quick. These methods are usually too risky and unlikely to be successful. Taking an approach where you are happy to leave your money to work for you over the years is the soundest approach. This is one reason why we have emphasized the need to set aside cash funds to avoid having to redeem investments at inopportune times.

Investing

To build your wealth, it is absolutely crucial that you learn to invest your money wisely. Obviously, any investment comes with some risk, and there is always a chance that you may fail to earn high returns. However, if you choose to invest wisely, you have higher chances of not only recouping your money but making a lot more. This will enable you to grow your wealth, save for retirement, and achieve your long-term financial goals.

So, how do you know when you are ready to invest?

Well, here are some signs that help you determine whether you are in a position to start investing:

i) You Have Enough Savings to Cater for Emergency Costs

Before you begin investing, you should ensure that you have some savings in a bank account to meet any unplanned expenses that may arise. For instance, you may find yourself in a situation where you suddenly need to fix your car battery due to unforeseen damage or repair a roof, which has started leaking. Having emergency savings to meet these costs will help you to avoid scenarios where you are forced to sell off your assets to raise money to cover these costs.

ii) You have Paid Off Your High-Interest Debts

If you decide to invest in the stock market, you may earn an interest of 8 - 10 percent, which is a fairly good return on investment. However, it may still be quite low when compared with some high-interest debt that you may have on car loans and even credit card debt. Since you will end up paying a lot more on interest than you will earn from investing, it makes more sense to pay off these debts first before you start investing.

iii) You have Extra Cash Every Month

If you always end up with leftover cash after covering your living costs and other non-recurring expenses such as property taxes and vehicle insurance, then you may be in a good position to start investing. One way to tell whether you have surplus cash to put into investments is to check your savings account. If the money is piling up every month, this is a good indicator that you are ready to invest.

iv) You Have a Basic Knowledge of how Investing Works

You certainly don't need to be Jeff Bezos or Elon Musk to start investing. However, you should have a basic understanding of the rudiments of investing. This includes knowing how assets and stocks work. Furthermore, you need to have an inclination to learn more about the world of investing to expand your knowledge. This will help you become better at identifying investment opportunities and making the right decisions.

What Should You Invest In?

Once you have determined that you are in a position to begin investing, the next step is to figure out where to invest. Fortunately, there are lots of great investment opportunities, which can provide you with good returns for your money even if you only have a small amount to invest. These include:

i) The Stock Market(s)

The stock market is, without a doubt, one of the best places to invest your hard-earned cash, especially if you put your money into exchange-traded funds (ETFs). These allow you to quickly own a variety of financial assets such as stocks at a low cost while also enabling you to get exposure to different areas of the market. This reduces market volatility and risk, making them a great investment for beginners.

Over long periods, the stock markets(s) generally beat property and bonds as an investment class. However, they are more volatile (they go up and back down, sometimes violently), and you have to be ready to ride these gyrations without losing your nerve.

ii) Investment Bonds

When you purchase bonds, you are essentially lending money to a company or the government, for which you are entitled to receive interest on the loan until the bond matures. This is a lower risk investment opportunity, which allows you to grow your income, albeit at a slower rate since bonds generally attract little interest. Generally, the better the return on the bond, the riskier it will be.

iii) Property

People love investing in property because they understand it, and it is real; a physical, tangible asset you can touch. However, it is not without risk. It would be rare to be able to buy an entire property outright, so most people have to borrow money to find the purchase and only put in a deposit. This is called leverage. It can generate very high returns, but it is not without its risks, and if you cannot keep up the payments, you may lose 100% of your investment. *(This is highly, highly unlikely in an ETF).*

TABLE: PERFORMANCE OF BONDS VS STOCKS

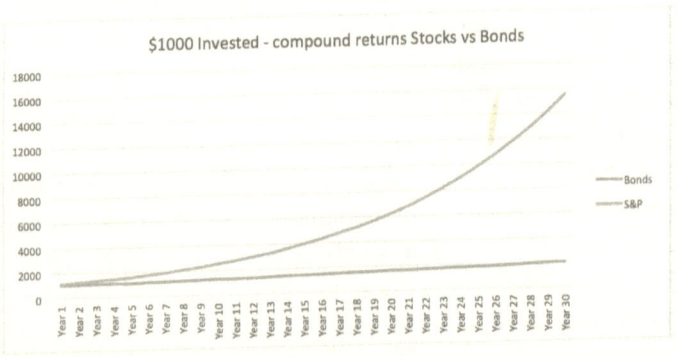

The table above shows the relative performance of $1,000 invested in stocks versus bonds over 30 years (the typical life of a mortgage). This uses the historic average performance of the S&P 500 over the past 50 years with 1% deducted for fees (9.57% average annual return). For bonds, the average performance is 2.4% adjusted for inflation. I was going to include gold in the comparison, but the wild gyrations in price and accounting for the costs of holding it made that difficult. For example, if you bought gold in 1980 you would still be sitting on a sizable loss forty years later. If you bought it in 2000 (at a low of $388) and held it till now you would have achieved approximately 338% return, which is respectable. The local nature of the property market also makes like-for-like comparison rather meaningless. Obviously some people swear by property investment, but the statistics tend to favor shares over a long period.

Use Tax-Free Investment to build Wealth

One of the most important lessons of wealth building is to exploit to the maximum all the different methods of saving and investing that are either free from tax or sheltered from tax. The reasons for this are common sense. All things being equal investments that can be made free of tax (that is to say from your gross earnings, such as 401k contributions) benefit from an immediate boost in their return equivalent to the tax rate. That is like giving your money a (near) 30% shot in the arm.

The effect of putting money in tax-free is the equivalent of turbocharging an engine, except that an engine eventually hits a maximum power output, where your investments have no upper limit. This means that the 'magic' compounding effect will over 30 years take $1,000 and turn it into $2,100, whereas paying that tax then investing what remains (assumed $720) would only be $1,444. That gap only gets bigger over time, all other things being equal. See the table below.

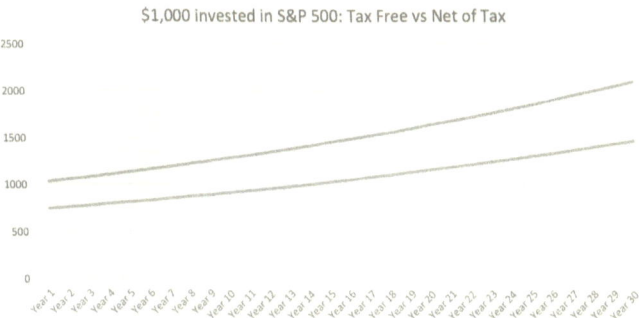

Tax-Free investments UK & US

Note that not all investments that are "free" of tax allow you to save from gross (before tax) income. Many schemes apply only to net (after-tax) income but after that allow capital growth, interest, and/or dividends to be tax-free. The table below shows (some) of the most common options.

Tax Status	US Tax exempt	UK Tax exempt
Contributions gross & Tax exempt	401(k)/403(b) Employer-Sponsored Retirement Plan	SIPP, Personal Pension or Employer Pension scheme
Contributions net but thereafter tax exempt	Traditional IRA/Roth IRA	ISA (Cash or share)
Contributions gross & Tax exempt, with restrictions	Health Savings Account (HSA)	
Contributions net but thereafter tax exempt	Municipal Bonds	UK Gilts / treasury stock
Contributions net but thereafter tax exempt	Tax-free Exchange Traded Funds (ETF)	
Contributions net but thereafter tax exempt	529 Education Fund	Children's ISA
Contributions net but thereafter tax exempt	U.S. Series I Savings Bond	Premium bonds and National Savings

Cost Averaging

I would like to explain what the S&P 500 index is, as we have been using it as a benchmark.

Basically, the Standard & Poors 500 Index is a collection of stocks that reflects the characteristics of the (New York) stock market as a whole. The stocks that make up the S&P 500 are selected by market capitalization, liquidity (volume of shares traded), and industry. This is why it is frequently used as a comparator and proxy for the performance of the whole market.

One of the reasons why people are afraid of investing in the stock market is the propensity for it to "crash". Periodically the value of investments held in stocks and shares will go through a major correction - that is fall in value by over 20%. However, it should be noted that most of these falls follow on from a period of sustained growth so that often the market is higher at the end than it was after the previous fall. Thus over a longer time-frame, the stock market, as represented by the S&P 500 has risen. However, year on year growth can swing wildly *(see the table below)*, and this is why I want to tell you about cost averaging.

S&P 500 ACTUAL YEARLY RETURNS

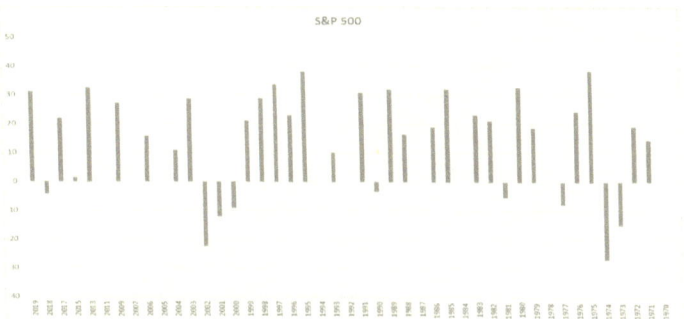

The concept of cost averaging is simple; it is the antithesis of trying to judge when we should buy or sell the market. If you make regular (smaller) investments into the market, then you will buy at an average price, sometimes higher and sometimes lower, but you won't try to second guess the market. Even investment professionals are notorious for failing to beat the market performance consistently. By making regular investments, then you will be using cost averaging to smooth out your returns, making them as effective as possible.

Many saving schemes are set up to allow you to invest like this with modest sums. The second advantage of using this method is that your money immediately goes to work for you, and if you were to try and wait for a market fall, then you could wait years. Even then, you can miss the opportunity by waiting to see if it will fall further. Essentially this approach avoids the issue with human psychology, which means that most people will buy at the top and sell at the bottom of the market.

Investing small amounts regularly *(for many years)* is the most reliable way to build real wealth.

3 Rules of Investing

1. **Start today:** The earlier you start, the longer your money will have to work for you, the more work that compounding will do.
2. **Stay disciplined and focused:** Increase your contributions to your investments as fast as you are able. Take full advantage of any pension match schemes. Don't be tempted to cash in retirement plans when you switch jobs - move them to a new plan if you are allowed.
3. **Be patient**: Do not panic if your investment falls, things will even out. Just ride the market and don't check on things too often. Being a passive investor is usually the best strategy. I have made some of my biggest mistakes by trying to time market falls. Conversely, some of my biggest successes are passively investing over many years in the way I have just described.

By taking advantage of these and more investment opportunities, you can put your money to good use and earn returns on your investments, which will help you to grow your income and achieve your financial goals. As we conclude this chapter, it is worth remembering that prosperity is always relative to what is around you. So, if you can maintain savings equivalent to 3-6 months of your expenses, you are significantly better off than a large percentage of Americans and well on your way to achieving financial prosperity.

In summary, here are the crucial points to take away from this chapter:

- Ensure that you are ready to commit to investing. Having a Murphy fund and emergency fund shields you from any crisis in the event of unplanned expenses and emergencies
- You need to always maintain an emergency fund equal to 3-6 months of your total spending to have a safety net when unexpected events which require money arise
- Investing will help you to grow your income and achieve the financial goals that you have set for yourself, including a comfortable retirement and long-term financial success.
- Try to widen the gap between what you save and what you spend.
- Invest small amounts regularly and be patient. Ride out any market turbulence without selling your investments.

AFTERWORD

The journey to achieving financial freedom and success is not an easy one, and there are always obstacles along the way which threaten to stop you even before you start. However, the biggest of all these challenges is our mindset and the way we think about money.

In the ultra-materialistic world that we live in, there is always pressure for us to put up a front of wealth and extravagance even when we clearly can't afford it. The YOLO ethos has made us victims of unconstrained spending as we seek instant self-gratification at the expense of our futures. It is no wonder then that many people, including many high earners, find themselves stuck in a vicious cycle of paycheck-to-paycheck living and debt as they try to create the impression of wealth without anything tangible to back it up.

In addition, we have explored the issue of debt, which is one of the major challenges that many people often experience when trying to organize their finances. If you borrow money or take out loans to furnish an expensive lifestyle that your income cannot support, you are likely to sink into bad debt. This will not only cost you lots of dollars in interest over long periods but also keep you stuck in poverty as you spend a huge portion of your income to service these loans.

In this book, I have attempted to discuss how our spending habits keep us perpetually broke and show the ways in which one can turn the psychological tables toward intrinsic motivation, using our internal values rather than comparing ourselves with other people. We have discussed how adopting the stoic philosophy leads us to a more rewarding and virtuous lifestyle. With these ideas as our armor, we can defend ourselves from the constant pressures of materialism and break out of this financial 'cage' to achieve real prosperity.

We have also covered some of the challenges that may be holding you back from setting and pursuing your goals, as well as how to overcome them so that you can move forward. I have no doubt now that you are able to create meaningful goals that will not only help to improve your financial situation but also better your quality of life.

Another key area that we have covered is budgeting, and why it is always important to create and adhere to a budget. We have seen how useful a budget can be as a tool for curbing bad spending habits and creating healthy ones - *which will help you to increase your income and achieve your objectives, including saving and investing.* By applying the strategies that we have expounded, you can regain control of your money and become empowered to make better financial decisions that will keep you on the right track as you pursue your goals in life.

As we have seen from this book, an emergency fund or rainy day fund should be a fundamental part of your financial planning. Due to the unpredictable nature of life, there are times when unexpected events will arise, which require you to spend money that you had not planned on spending. This can be anything from a dental procedure *(which you suddenly need to undergo),* an unexpected expense arising from home repairs, or any other event that you did not anticipate. Without an emergency fund to meet these unexpected costs, you may find yourself in a very difficult financial situation, which may prompt you to take on an extra debt burden even when you don't want to. It is therefore important to have a safety net that can help you meet these costs comfortably, and that's what an emergency fund does for you.

Finally, we have explored the value of investing and why you should make it a priority to invest any extra cash that you have after covering your expenses. This not only allows you to grow your income but can help you to achieve your financial goals, such as retiring comfortably a lot faster.

I am confident that all the techniques, strategies, and practical wisdom that I have conveyed in this book will be of great value to you as you strive to live within your means and pursue your financial goals. The one thing I would like you to take away from this book is the consolation that however messed up your financial life may seem to be, you hold the power to turn things around and change your financial situation for the better. However, for you to create the future that you desire, you need to begin right now.

If you have already decided to transcend the perpetually broke lifestyle and create a better future for yourself and your family, **now** is the time to come up with a solid plan of action that will lift you out of financial straits and put you squarely on the path towards financial prosperity.

AUTHOR'S NOTE

Thank you for reading my book. I very much hope you enjoyed it and found it informative. It has taken a little longer and more work to put together than I imagined, and sometimes it is difficult to know when to stop, but I wanted to keep it on-point, as personal finance is such a big topic.

Anyway, I hope that you could now give me some indication of how well I achieved this by leaving me a review. Without reviews, my work will vanish without a trace, never to be seen by the world. I realize that this requires some effort on your part but just two minutes (to give one or two points on your impression and a rating) would be very helpful both to develop as an author and - hopefully - provide some satisfaction of a job well done.

I would like to help Tom by leaving a review

Thanks
    Tom Cromwell

THE PERSONAL FINANCIAL CALCULATOR - BUDGETING TOOL

(Never budget without this)

Save massive time and effort:

- Track your income and spending.
- Pre-configured with **21** critical budget categories.
- Calculate whether you have surplus or deficit, and track your savings.

The last thing you want is to miss critical items of expenditure that will ruin your budget because you forgot about them. I will also give you an additional 7 monster money tips.

To receive your **FREE** personal financial calculator & 7 monster money-saving tips, visit the link:

<u>www.personalfinancewizard.com</u>

REFERENCES

10 Benefits of Budgeting Your Money. (2017, April 15). Retrieved from https://www.budgetingincome.com/10-benefits-of-budgeting-your-money/

Bieber, C. (2019, May 11). Most Americans Run Out of Money Before Payday -- Here's What to Do If You're One of Them. Retrieved from https://www.fool.com/personal-finance/2019/05/11/most-americans-run-out-of-money-before-payday-here.aspx

Burton, N. (2018, September 17). 8 Warning Signs You're Living Beyond Your Means. Retrieved from https://www.hermoney.com/invest/financial-planning/warning-signs-of-living-beyond-your-means/

Chua, C. (2018, August 15). 7 Important Reasons Why You Should Set Goals. Retrieved from https://personalexcellence.co/blog/why-set-goals/

Edwards, D. (2009, June 29). The Addiction of Overspending. Retrieved from https://theoakstreatment.com/blog/addiction-of-overspending/

Fay, B. (2019, April 2). Good Debt vs. Bad Debt - Types of Good and Bad Debts. Retrieved from https://www.debt.org/advice/good-vs-bad/

Hamm, T. (2016, July 11). How the Principles of Stoicism Can Help Your Personal and Financial Life. Retrieved from https://lifehacker.com/how-the-principles-of-stoicism-can-help-your-personal-a-1783277251

Hill, D. (n.d.). 5 Reasons Getting Rich Quick Is Unlikely and Always Will Be. Retrieved June 10, 2020, from https://www.wisebread.com/5-reasons-getting-rich-quick-is-unlikely-and-always-will-be

How to Create Better Spending Habits. (n.d.). Retrieved June 10, 2020, from https://www.everydollar.com/blog/create-better-spending-habits

Maltz, M. (2015). Psycho-Cybernetics, Updated and expanded. Tarcher-Perigree books

O'Shea, B. (2020, January 16). Budgeting 101: How to Create a Budget. Retrieved from https://www.nerdwallet.com/blog/finance/how-to-build-a-budget/

Rains, J. (2020, February 14). 7 Signs You're Ready to Invest. Retrieved from https://investingtothrive.com/7-signs-you-are-ready-to-invest/

Rose, J. (2018, September 19). 8 Grown-Up Money Behaviors Keeping You Broke. Retrieved from https://www.forbes.

com/sites/jrose/2018/09/18/8-grown-up-money-behaviors-keeping-you-broke/#5b767add4d6e

Sheffield, T. (2019, September 24). 11 Ways To Stay Motivated & Focused To Achieve Your Goals. Retrieved from https://www.bustle.com/articles/172824-11-ways-to-stay-motivated-focused-to-achieve-your-goals

Smartsheet. (n.d.). The Essential Guide to Writing SMART Goals. Retrieved June 10, 2020, from https://www.smartsheet.com/blog/essential-guide-writing-smart-goals

Sokunbi, B. (2020, April 13). 10 Reasons Why You're Always Broke and How to Start Building Wealth Instead. Retrieved from https://www.clevergirlfinance.com/blog/why-youre-always-broke-how-to-build-wealth/

The Power of Publicly Committing to Your Goals -. (2017, September 27). Retrieved from https://www.antoinetteoglethorpe.com/power-of-public-commitment/

von Ahn, T. (2019, June 17). What Is Zero-Based Budgeting? Pros and Cons and How to Start. Retrieved from https://viralsolutions.net/what-is-zero-based-budgeting-pros-and-cons/#.XtS4hDpKjMw

What Debt Do You Pay Off First? (n.d.). Retrieved June 10, 2020, from https://www.everydollar.com/blog/what-debt-do-i-pay-off-first

What is Budgeting and Why is it Important? (n.d.). Retrieved June 10, 2020, from https://www.mymoneycoach.ca/budgeting/what-is-a-budget-planning-forecasting

www.ingramcontent.com/pod-product-compliance
Lightning Source LLC
Chambersburg PA
CBHW031628210526
45464CB00004B/1799